CW00554244

Thomas Johnston

Thomas Johnston

Graham Walker

Manchester University Press
Manchester and New York

Distributed exclusively in the USA and Canada by St. Martin's Press, New York

Copyright © Graham Walker 1988

Published by Manchester University Press, Oxford Road,
Manchester, M13 9PL, UK
and Room 400, 175 Fifth Avenue, New York, NY 10010, USA

Distributed exclusively in the USA and Canada
by St. Martin's Press, Inc., 175 Fifth Avenue, New York, NY 10010, USA

British Library cataloguing in publication data
Walker, Graham
    Thomas Johnston. — (Lives of the left)
    1. Great Britain. Politics. Johnston, Thomas, 1881-1965
    I. Title   II. Series
    941.082'09'4

Library of Congress cataloging in publication data
Walker, Graham
    Thomas Johnston / Graham Walker.
    p.cm. — (Lives of the left)
    Includes index.
    ISBN 0-7190-1996-6: $35.00 (U.S.: est.).
    ISBN 0-7190-1997-4 (pbk.): $12.00 (U.S.: est.)
    1. Johnston, Thomas, b. 1882. 2. Politicians—Scotland—Biography.
    3. Journalists—Scotland—Biography. 4. Scotland—Politics and
    government—20th century.
    I. Title   II. Series
    DA822.J6W34 1988
    941.'082'092'4—dc19

ISBN 0 7190 1996 6 *hardback*
ISBN 0 7190 1997 4 *paperback*

Set in Perpetua
by Koinonia Ltd, Manchester

Printed in Great Britain
by Robert Hartnoll (1985) Ltd, Bodmin, Cornwall

Contents

Acknowledgements

I am grateful for the encouragement and helpful co-operation which I received at the start of this project from the series editor, David Howell, Mr Don Martin of the William Patrick Memorial Library, Kirkintilloch, and Mrs Mary Knox.

Denis Cosgrove kindly secured me a recording of a valuable BBC Radio programme on Johnston written by Professor Chris Harvie, whose own work on Johnston and on Scottish affairs generally was a great source of inspiration. I also derived benefit from conversations with Tom Gallagher, Callum Brown, Alistair Dunnett, George Peden and John Vincent. None of them, of course, bear responsibility for the views advanced here.

The staffs of the various archives and libraries I worked in were helpful and courteous, and I particularly thank those connected with the Glasgow Room of the Mitchell Library.

Research for the book was assisted by grants from the Scottish Arts Council and the Twenty-Seven Foundation.

I am grateful, finally, to my parents for the vividness of their wartime memories, and, once more, for their support.

1 First steps forward (1881-1914)

'. . . he was the greatest Scotsman of modern times, and the one who did most for his country' (*The Scotsman*, 6 September 1965).

Such extravagant praise has been offered rarely in modern Scotland, a land of 'precious few heroes'.[1] The Jacobite tendency to romanticise failure has probably made a deeper impact on recent popular consciousness than celebration of isolated successes. Thomas Johnston is widely viewed as one such success. His achievements were tangible; they commanded respect and admiration. His name can evoke a sense of pride which rises above mere sentimentality. A quietly formidable man has spawned a legend in his own image.

I

He was born on 2 November 1881 at Kirkintilloch in Dunbartonshire, the eldest child of David Johnston, a licensed victualler, and his wife Mary Blackwood. His upbringing was a comfortable one materially, and his education relatively privileged. Thomas Johnston attended Lairdslaw Public School and Lenzie Academy, the latter an institution of some repute. By his own account he received a sound grounding in the classics, especially the history of Ancient Greece and Rome.[2] Even at this early stage Johnston's enthusiasm for history and for creative writing became apparent. As a schoolboy he enjoyed success in essay competitions, and had his own stories published in boys' comic books. The 'scribbling itch' was to be the main motivating force of his life.

His formative influences offered no hint of his adult political destination. In his teenage years Johnston echoed the Tory views of his family, and reviled Gladstone, Home Rule and the Income Tax.[3] This might have reflected the notable middle-class drift in Scotland in the late 1880s and 1890s from Liberalism to Conservatism (or Unionism), a phenomenon largely created by the traumatic effect of the Irish Home Rule issue. However, Liberalism was still by far the most dominant political force in the Scotland of Johnston's youth, based as it was on religious, democratic and land reform factors which distinguished the Scottish political world from that of the rest of the United Kingdom. Educational influences and a small-town environment would also have made the young Johnston familiar with Liberal nostrums of self-help and individual responsibility, values which at the time were generally ranged against the emerging socialist movement. In such communities as Johnston's socialist agitators were likely to be viewed as 'on the make'.

Kirkintilloch was a burgh of ancient pedigree. As a community it had existed in pre-Roman times, long before Glasgow appeared just south of it on the map. The town itself grew up around the site of a fort on Antonine's wall. With the remains of the Roman conquest on his doorstep, it is perhaps not surprising that Johnston grew up with a sharp sense of historical enquiry. He certainly immersed himself in the history and folklore of his home town, and the proximity of the surrounding countryside encouraged in him a love of leisure pursuits such as fishing. Small-town life in such an inspiriting rural setting defined for Johnston a life-long aversion to urban conglomerations.

By the turn of the century Johnston had become receptive to the socialist ideas he had been earlier encouraged to disparage. The change seems to have occurred at a time of personal uncertainty and frustration. On leaving school he had found work as a clerk, first in an iron-founding business, and subsequently in law and insurance offices. The work did not enthral him, and

Johnston's enquiring mind and desire to write for a living led him towards politics and the activities of the Fabian Society and the Independent Labour Party (ILP). Keir Hardie, already a venerable symbol of Labour and socialist politics, was an important influence. Hardie at this time edited the socialist newspaper, *Labour Leader*, which conveyed the kind of crusading zeal which appealed to someone of Johnston's temperament, background and rapidly developing sense of social justice. *Labour Leader* was serious, it extolled the virtues of Christian socialism, and it condemned decadence, moral impurity and corruption.[4] To all this Johnston responded readily, and from it he derived much inspiration in respect of his own career designs.

In 1903 Johnston stood for election as an ILP candidate for the Kirkintilloch School Board. He won a seat and took his first tentative step into public life at the age of twenty one. After some notable attempts to extend the range of the Board's evening classes for adults, he resigned in 1906 following the setting up of new School Management Committees. However, in the same year, he fell heir to a distant relative's printing establishment. The way was now clear to wed his journalistic ambitions to his socialist convictions.

II

Johnston decided, along with some Fabian friends, to launch a Socialist weekly newspaper, the *Forward*. The paper first appeared on 13 October 1906. It was able to get off the ground largely through the financial backing of Roland Muirhead, a wealthy tanner who was a Scottish Home Ruler first and a Fabian Socialist second. Muirhead was to come to the paper's rescue several times in its early years as it hovered on the edge of bankruptcy. Muirhead's generosity notwithstanding, *Forward* was a genuinely independent venture. While it came to be closely associated with the ILP in Scotland, it was no mere party mouthpiece.

3

Johnston assumed the editorship and determined, virtually single-handedly, the paper's style and character. Like *Labour Leader* it was, first and foremost, a serious propaganda tool in the cause of socialism. Johnston echoed Hardie's puritan strain: he refused to accept alcohol advertisements and carried no gambling news. Johnston was himself a teetotaller, in spite of his father's trade. *Forward*'s first priority was to educate; almost everything that appeared in the paper was for a political or educational purpose.

However, the paper was neither dogmatic nor dull. Johnston ensured from the beginning that its columns would be open to a range of different viewpoints – some decidedly hostile to socialism and the Labour movement. 'The *Forward*', he stated in the prospectus circulated to publicise its arrival, 'will be non-sectarian and non-bigot. Progressive thought is wide in its sweep, and Truth arises from the clash of opinions. The unpopular will not be boycotted because of its unpopularity.'[5] Johnston thus encouraged open debate and set a tolerant and reasonable editorial tone, even if some of his own contributions to debates were somewhat brusque. He also realised that for the paper to be a commercial success it had to have an accessible and appealing style. *Forward*, in this respect, owed more to Robert Blatchford's *Clarion* than to Hardie's *Labour Leader*. Johnston himself was a skilled polemicist – 'a master of the short pithy paragraph and the acid phrase'.[6] *Forward*'s way of entertaining, however, was to feature humorous, satirical articles with a clear political message. Unlike Blatchford, Johnston had no time for popular amusement and sport for their own sake. Indeed, he consistently viewed such aspects of working-class culture as damaging distractions to the work of the Labour movement. *Forward*'s contributors, from its earliest days, were as diverse as the views represented in its pages: Marxists like John MacLean, anti-Marxists like Dr Stirling Robertson ('Rob Roy'), the literary giants H. G. Wells and Bernard Shaw, and Parliamentary Labour spokesmen such

4

as Ramsay MacDonald and Keir Hardie himself.

Given his purposeful editorial style and formidable journalistic ability, it was inevitable that *Forward*, to some extent, would be a vehicle for Johnston's own brand of socialism. In the paper's early years this meant a general commitment to the gradualism of the British Labour Party, spiced with some evangelical urgency typical of the ILP.

Johnston supported the Parliamentary Labour Party – which was thirty strong after the 1906 election – critically. In the third issue of *Forward* he sharply rebuked Ramsay MacDonald for boasting about the 'respectablity' of the Labour Party.[7] For Johnston, the Labour Party was at Westminster to preach the socialist message in the most strident terms. On several occasions in the period 1906-10 he censured the Labour MPs for not making nuisances of themselves. Such attacks reached a peak in 1909 when Johnston's accusations of supine behaviour on the part of Labour MPs drew a challenging response from Joseph Duncan, a prominent Aberdeen trade unionist and ILP figure. Duncan questioned Johnston's advocacy of 'disturbance tactics', and called on him to lay down a clear line of policy. Johnston replied with a list of obstructionist tactics reminiscent of the heyday of Parnell and the Irish Party. Johnston's concern to foster a 'spirit of revolt' in the Labour Party at this time thus brought him to a position of ambivalence regarding parliamentary procedures and conventions. However, he was careful that the balance never tipped too far away from the ultimate commitment to electoral and parliamentary methods. 'Revolt' was always to be within a framework of accepted rules.

Johnston was almost definitively a creature of the ILP. He believed implicitly in the eventual triumph of socialism; it had to come because it was ethical. Johnston viewed socialism as resting on ethical foundations rather than the theoretical abstractions of thinkers such as Marx. For Johnston, the necessity of

5

socialism sprang from the 'instinct of beauty ... the instinct of self-preservation ... the social needs of mankind'.[8] He viewed society as evolving towards such a condition and saw no need to overturn existing institutions to hasten the process. Nothing in the constitution, in Johnston's view, prevented the coming of socialism. The key lay in educating the workers as to their class interests. The workers, Johnston believed, would bring about socialism when they were ready to do so. In essentials Johnston's outlook was that of Ramsay Macdonald and the Fabians. But Johnston was perhaps more alive to the variety of potential ways in which Labour leaders could educate and inspire and arouse class-consciousness.

Moreover, Johnston stood apart from those Fabians and ILPers who disavowed class conflict.[9] If he was content to leave 'class war' rhetoric to the Marxists of the Social Democratic Federation (SDF), he nonetheless defined political issues consistently in class terms. While his learned colleague on *Forward*, 'Rob Roy', was advancing qualified praise of the Liberal Government's social welfare reforms, Johnston preferred to remind the readership that the Liberals were at root a party of the capitalist class whose interests were inimical to those of the mass of the people. Johnston considered such social reforms as old-age pensions as valuable gains for the working class. He frequently disparaged the 'theory of increasing misery' which he accused Marxist Socialists such as John MacLean of holding. Johnston believed that the more such gains were made by the working class, the better equipped they would be to fight for socialism. He saw no discrepancy between this belief and the simultaneous assertion that such measures represented the 'ambulance work' of capitalism.

If Johnston could see no way of avoiding class conflict, he could see many strategies of waging it for the benefit of the working class. What was important to him was the choice of the right tactics for the right issues and situations. In response, for example, to the wave of strikes in the summer of 1910, Johnston counselled against such action pre-empting political activity. He wrote: 'We must educate . . . and in all our education endeavour to escape the falsity of extremes. The useful is the good – so far we are Pragmatists – and we shall live to find all methods useful, from the staid political manoeuvre to the boycott and the national strike, from the 'Gas and Water' Socialist experiment to the Hunger March.'[10]

III

Forward arrived at a momentous time. Edwardian Britain was a society in ferment, and great political issues began to unfold dramatically. The sweeping nature of the Liberals' election triumph in 1906 perhaps suggested that the country was ready for change. Victorian certainties had evaporated. A mood of restlessness was soon to bring very real social and political instability.

Johnston, through the medium of his paper and Labour public meetings, addressed himself to the questions of the day. He backed the women's suffrage cause vigorously and upbraided those males in the Labour movement who equivocated. For Johnston, the fact that many adult males were still deprived of the vote was not an argument for preventing women achieving it on the same limited terms.[11] He also dealt scathingly with protectionist arguments, espcially when they were linked to social reform. Welfare schemes, Johnston argued, could be paid for by graduated income tax. Nationalisation schemes – of the railways, the mines and the land – were rehearsed regularly in *Forward*, and were viewed by Johnston as one of the few objectives worth calling a general strike for. Johnston also published, along with a colleague, a cogently argued pamphlet on railway nationalisation.[12] Municipalisation was a *cause célèbre*, the more so since

7

Johnston could point to successful schemes such as the Glasgow tramways. Moreover, he was quick to answer right-wing charges that socialist municipal schemes would increase the rates. To Johnston it was obvious that better and cheaper housing would go a long way to solving health and social problems. The heavy burden that hospitals, the poor law, the police and such like put on the rates would thus be reduced.

But Johnston was by no means narrowly political in his concerns. In 1907 he entered Glasgow University for the first of two sessions, studying Moral Philosophy and Political Economy. He studied under Professor Henry Jones and Professor William Smart respectively, and revelled in sparring verbally with the former. His philosophical training found expression in *Forward* where he published series of articles on the meaning of liberty, freedom and the law, and 'socialism and genius'. In the latter articles Johnston argued vigorously that indvidual talent would flourish as never before under socialism. This was perhaps an attempt to tap into the strong vein of individualism in the Scottish consciousness. Socialism, Johnston stressed, did not imply regimental conformity. University education probably also rendered Johnston more sure of himself in the theoretical controversies he occasionally embarked upon, such as the issue of socialism in relation to Christianity. This was a topic all the more pertinent to Johnston for those elements in Scottish religious life which seemed to harmonise with his socialist outlook. Such elements centred on the democratic tradition in Scottish Presbyterianism and the aura of solemn dignity with which men were held to be equal before God. Just as Presbyterian beliefs had shaped a more egalitarian education system in Scotland than in England, so Johnston hoped that they might embrace a wider creed of social justice and equality for society as a whole.

Johnston entered fully into university life, and was responsible for forming a socialist society which promptly nominated Keir

Hardie for rector. A rumbustious campaign was fought but Hardie could poll only 123 votes. Two contemporaries of Johnston's at the unversity were later to feature prominently in his political life: James Maxton, then a Tory, and Walter Elliot, then a Fabian Socialist. Johnston left university in 1909 without a degree.

The specific issue which most exercised Johnston's mind in this period was that of land reform. In June 1908 he published in the *Forward* the first in a long series of articles on 'Our Scots Noble Families'. The articles were the fruit of many hours of careful research on local records in many parts of Scotland. They presented to the readers of *Forward* a weekly digest of aristocratic plunder, and were penned in an unashamedly inflammatory style. 'We', he wrote in the first instalment, 'who think that the land should be owned by the State, we who think that no one man has a right to enclosure fields for sport while other men starve by the wayside for lack of food, we who *know* that the lands of Britain belong to the Crown (and through the Crown to the people), we who know that the land has been pillaged and stolen by ducal brigands, we who still pay rents to the descendants of these brigands, we who are chased from the mountain sides by their keepers and from the burn-sides by their water-baliffs – we, are *we* the Robbers?'[13]

The articles were collected and published in book form in 1909. The volume constituted one of the most searing assaults on the landed class ever written. It was propaganda of the most febrile kind, redolent both of the old-fashioned radical liberal school and the Scottish theological pamphlet literature of the eighteenth and early nineteenth centuries. Moreover, it appeared as the debate on Lloyd George's 'People's budget' was taking place, and with the storm over his Limehouse speech still reverberating. As such, as Ramsay Macdonald said in his preface, it was a powerful answer to the accusations of theft and robbery then being made by landowners. For the latter to speak of land taxation and compulsory land purchase as injustice was, for Mac-Donald, 'nothing but impertinence and hypocrisy'. *Our Scots Noble Families'* sold out rapidly and was to go through several editions. In all it was to sell over 100,000 copies. It boosted too the sales and reputation of *Forward*, and put Johnston in the front rank of British Labour propagandists.

However, Johnston's objectives in writing such a philippic went much further than personal gratification. He wanted primarily to fuel the campaign for land reform in Scotland which aimed to buy out the existing landlords and create smallholdings to bring people back to the Highlands. The land would thus be returned to the people. But Johnston realised that there was again a huge educational task in front of him. *Our Scots Noble Families* was therefore designed to do a debunking job: 'to show the people that our Old Nobility is not noble, that lands are stolen lands – stolen either by force or fraud ... dissolve the halo of divinity that surrounds the heriditary title ... do these things and you shatter the Romance that keeps the nation dumb and spellbound while privilege picks its pockets'.

The book was only, in Johnston's term, the 'precursor' of an organisation which he helped to establish at this juncture. This was the Highland Land League (HLL) which was launched in August 1909. The HLL, on the face of it, stood for the return of the land to the people and the return to parliament of men in sympathy with such an aspiration. For Johnston, however, it was also to be the means of linking the Labour movement with the rural population: an alliance of crofters and cottars with industrial urban workers in a new radically-conscious Scotland. Johnston took the view that the Labour and socialist movement had hitherto been negligent of rural constituencies, and had failed to develop a proper policy towards land problems. He wanted specifically to see Labour breaking the Liberal stranglehold in the crofting communities of the Highlands.

Johnston, besides becoming Vice-President of the HLL, thus ensured that a clause be put in the Constitution to the effect that new candidates who stood for election with the League's support had also to be Labour Party members. The President of the HLL was Dr G. B. Clark, the former crofters' MP for Caithness, who had recently transferred his political allegiance from the Liberals to Labour. Nevertheless, Johnston's identification of the ILP in Scotland with the HLL caused some disquiet. George Dallas, the Secretary of the Scottish ILP Federation, objected to ILP speakers, including Johnston, sharing a platform with pro-land Reform Liberals at a meeting on Glasgow Green in September 1909. Johnston retorted that the speakers would make it clear that they were in favour of the land clauses of Lloyd George's budget and not the budget in general. In the event Johnston used the meeting, and other HLL gatherings in the Highlands, to stress that there were other enemies as well as landlords. Land Reform, however, would in Johnston's view, be a potential catalyst to wider social change, 'the beginning of a new era'.[14]

This was pitching expectations rather high. The HLL certainly drew an enthusiastic response in the Highlands in the short term, but its impact proved to be ephemeral. The bulk of the Highland voters remained with the Liberals, despite Labour's close identification with the HLL. The League's main objective – nationalisation of the land – came no nearer to being realised. The HLL may have made more lowland urban workers aware of the struggle over land, but it roused few to more than passive sympathy.

Johnston certainly did his best to publicise the issue and to keep it at the top of the Scottish Labour movement's agenda. He did not stop at caustic attacks on landlords and stirring slogans. *Forward* carried long and detailed proposals about how the land could, step by step, be nationalised. Johnston strongly advocated the abolition of the law of Inheritance and Bequest:

'The real method of social salvation ... is by the abolition of hereditary transmission of social wealth from private owner to private owner. Let the present owner retain possession, let his son who has been brought up to believe that he would inherit, receive undisturbed possession, but let the son's son, yet unborn, enter life with the knowledge that he has a race to run ... The State must become residuary legatee.'[15] Johnston also pressed for the conversion of land used for sport (such as deer forests) into small crofter holdings, for laws compelling the production of title, and for large-scale afforestation of derelict land. The latter idea was one Johnston was to return to time and again during the course of his career. He saw the potential which afforestation schemes held for providing employment and stimulating paper mills and associated trades.

Johnston's commitment to the cause of land reform was absolute. It was no mere political stategy. He also wanted to see a repopulation of the Highlands and a revival of national pride. Both went hand in hand, for Johnston's vision of a revitalised Scotland was of a basically rural and small-town society. To Johnston, Scotland's democratic and egalitarian spirit rested in this type of environment. The anti-landlordism and Presbyterian radicalism of rural Scotland inspired him; it was all very redolent of a perceived tradition which had been forged by the Covenanters and personified by Robert Burns. This Scottish legend had great emotional significance for Johnston, as it had for Hardie and other Scottish Labour leaders.

But Johnston might also have been motivated to fight on land issues out of a species of urban phobia. He quite simply detested big-city life. An article in one of *Forward*'s earliest issues depicted the city as a claustrophobic and stultifying environment, the quality of its day-to-day life meretricious and hollow. Such a city was Glasgow – 'Glasgow where the lark sings but a month ere it dies, where the flowers, human and vegetable, sicken, wither and perish, where gusts of factory smoke swirl around corners, where the great bulk are poor, lacking in the only wealth, the joy of life.'[16] Again the style – and indeed content – of such writing was close to the radical liberal polemic of the day, such as that of Charles Masterman.

Johnston had no 'feel' for Glasgow working-class popular culture. He despised alcohol and pubs, although his regard for the Temperance movement itself was low. Popular pastimes and amusements, especially football and horse-racing, he could not view as in any way life-enhancing. Rural life, on the other hand, was healthy and invigorating in itself. Rural culture fostered at once a positive and responsible outlook on life. Johnston was certainly no killjoy and possessed a quite mischievous sense of humour. However, he considered the city's leisure aspects as monotonous and soulless as the drudgery of its work. Moreover, he believed that too many city workers used their leisure time to fight among themselves.

Johnston therefore turned to the land question almost in the spirit of escaping the city and its attendant social problems. The highlands had none of the problems which dogged the Labour movement in the city. As he put it in an article on the HLL: 'In the Highlands there is no Orange v. Green problem, no distracting music hall, but there is a deep-seated class hatred that unites even the parish kirk beadle and the Wee Free precentor in the common cause of seeing that no Tory gets within thousands of a Parliamentary majority.'[17]

There was a large element of truth in this, but it was romanticism nonetheless. It ignored the deeply conservative side to rural – and especially highland – Scottish life. It was naive in its apparent belief that such anti-landlordism or anti-Toryism was but a step from socialism, requiring only the right kind of leadership and organisation. Not least, it was a perilous attitude to adopt for a Labour spokesman; the city and its teeming mass of workers could not be wished away in flights of arcadian fancy.

Such rural romanticism, it should be said, was another strong feature of the ILP in Britain, and Johnston's rhapsodies were in line with the 'Merrie England' kind of socialist propaganda which lamented a lost world. But Johnston was blind to the vitality of the city; he saw only the squalor. In this he was very different from propagandists like Blatchford, and from leading Glasgow Socialists such as John Wheatley and Patrick Dollan, two contributors to *Forward*.

Johnston might be said to have had a 'block' when it came to the very poor of the cities. He certainly prided himself on producing a newspaper which was read by the respectable working class. Like a lot of Labour leaders in this period, Johnston raised surprisingly little fuss over the fact that so many poorer workers remained unenfranchised. Those who were at the bottom of the social scale he viewed with some despair, sceptical of the part some said they could be mobilised to play in the Labour movement. Johnston was not of course unsympathetic to their material plight. He simply believed that the Labour movement should target the better-off and better educated workers in the interests of building up a strong political force more rapidly. Only with the advance of Labour in this way could the wretched state of the poor be properly tackled. Too often, however, Johnston's romanticisation of rural life and praise for the 'responsible' working man could seem like an avoidance of problems which demanded to be priorities.

One aspect of Scottish urban working-class culture which particularly dismayed Johnston was religious sectarianism. The great bulk of Irish emigrants in the nineteenth century settled in Glasgow and West–Central Scotland. They formed a disproportinate part of the low-skilled working class and inhabited some of the poorest areas of the cities and towns. Their Roman Catholic religion – Irish Protestants also emigrated but in far fewer numbers – was the main barrier to their acceptance by the indigenous population. The competition for low-skilled jobs which they often caused was another. And, not least, the Irish organised themselves politically. The United Irish League (UIL) expertly marshalled the Catholic vote to the ends of Irish nationalism. In the early years of the twentieth century this meant conditional support for the Liberals. Labour faced the daunting task of breaking this arrangement and overcoming the anti-socialist hostility of the Catholic Church.

It also faced the problem of Protestant working-class sect-arianism, which manifested itself in the Orange Order. Orangeism was by this time an important social phenomenon in lowland Scotland. Politically, its impact was still uncertain, but there were clearly areas in Glasgow and in towns such as Motherwell where the 'Orange vote' went to the Conservatives (or Unionists). There were also Orange mob orators, like one Pastor Boal, whose fol-lowers wreaked havoc at ILP meetings in 1907 and 1908. The opposition to socialism on the part of Catholic prelates was no less damaging for being confined to words in the pulpit and press.

Johnston's own religious views do not seem to have been strong. His Presbyterian background instilled in him no love of Calvinism, which he berated in *Forward*. However, as has been noted, he did possess an affinity with the historically radical spirit of Scottish Presbyterianism. He had no sympathy with Orangeism, but he certainly tried to convince Orange workers that there was a way in which their Protestant heritage and beliefs could find expression through socialism. This was perhaps designed to balance Scottish Labour support for Irish Home Rule.

On the Catholic side, Johnston gave generous space in *Forward* to the affairs of the Catholic Socialist Society (CSS) which had been set up in Glasgow in 1906 by John Wheatley. This society attempted to convince Catholic workers that *their* religious beliefs were not incompatible with socialism. The CSS, after a stormy first couple of years, began to make significant progress in this direction. However, Johnston's own view of the Catholic Church seems always to have been tinged with suspicion. In this period he certainly did not hesitate to condemn what he saw as its lack of concern for the poverty of many of its flock. Johnston was also suspicious of the United Irish League and its *petit-bourgeois* leadership, many of whom were in the drink trade. In 1911 he strongly criticised the Calton ILP branch in Glasgow for supporting, at a municipal election, an Irish publican who held anti-socialist views.

Religious sectarianism was thus a serious problem for the Labour movement in Scotland. However, when the Glasgow experience is compared to that of Belfast or even Liverpool, it is arguable that it was relatively well contained. Possible reasons for this have been cogently advanced by Joan Smith, who lays great stress on the strength of liberalism among Scottish artisans from the mid-nineteenth century. The Labour movement in Glasgow, she argues, built upon this tradition of 'liberal common-sense'. In addition, Protestant skilled workers faced relatively little Catholic competition for work in Glasgow. And, very importantly, residential segregation along religious lines does not seem to have been particularly marked in Glasgow.[18]

This still leaves the question of working-class Unionism in West–Central Scotland, a significant and growing force in the late nineteenth and early twentieth centuries. As David Howell has suggested, this was probably more *Unionist* than *Conservative*.[19] Notwithstanding Labour's pro-Home rule stance, it was quite feasible for Labour to cultivate support among such workers. For, arguably, much working-class Unionism was a complex mixture of Orangeism and liberal or even socialist radicalism. Much would depend on the resolution of the Irish issue in British politics. In the post-war years this question was to be of central importance to Labour's fortunes in Scotland.

IV

Johnston may have had his flushes of romanticism but he was at root a pragmatist. He had no illusions about the scale of the Labour movement's fundamental task: organisation. In September 1909 he launched a *Forward* 'organisation scheme' with these chastening words: 'Unless we are going in a body to the stairheads as per the scheme, for any sake let us keep back from the polls altogether. We can win seats if we like; but we won't win them by promiscuous indoor or outdoor cheering; and unless we are prepared to face the question of organisation in a rational, careful, determined plodding manner, we may as well give the booths a rest.'[20]

In the wake of the January 1910 election at which Labour won only two seats in Scotland, Johnston went on the offensive. He excoriated candidates for not getting themselves into the field until the election campaign was well under way; he pointed to the lack of registration and canvassing work and to poor sales and distribution of literature; and he scorned those who seemed to believe that enthusiastic meetings were all that was required to build up electoral support. He went on to urge prospective candidates to start immediately the work of organising and maintaining the organisation of the Party in their constituencies. Registration, canvassing and fund-raising, he stressed, had to be started there and then.

Johnston recognised, as some Labour activists did not, that the appearance of great activity and vitality belied inadequate organisational capabilities. The Labour movement in Scotland was still in reality a weak force. Trade union political involvement was only marginal, and many unions were themselves negligible in terms of numbers and financial resources. Not enough was being done to boost trade union membership and in turn to harness the unions effectively to the political movement. What

17

was also required was a well-drilled political machine to which trade union resources could be harnessed. Trade unionism in Scotland retained a sectionalist character based on a firm craft conservatism. This was largely unaltered by the 'New Unionism', and organisation among the semi-skilled and unskilled was piti-fully weak. The trade union profile in industrial Scotland was shadowy, and its bargaining muscle unimpressive.

Labour in Scotland, in a political sense, was essentially the ILP. By 1908 the ILP had 130 branches in Scotland and carried on an impressive range of activities. However, much of this centred on the 'promiscuous' type of propaganda, such as stirring oratory at public meetings, about which Johnston was lukewarm. He was firmly of the view that the production and distribution of literature was more important to party organisation: 'If you get Socialist thought, you'll get Socialist branches, and you'll get finance and enthusiasm and organisers . . .'[21] Too many activists preferred to ignore such advice and over-estimated their own powers of verbal persuasion. On the other hand, Johnston was well aware that, while he was a first-rate journalist, he was a mediocre public speaker.

It became clear in these years that sustaining a distinctively Scottish Labour identity would be problematic. The organisation in Scotland of the Labour Party itself suffered from the legacy of earlier friction between the Labour Representation Committee (LRC) and the Scottish Workers' Parliamentary Election Com-mittee (SWPEC – formed in 1900). This concerned differences over the issue of exactly what the two committees were respon-sible for, and led to quarrels over the financial contributions of the SWPEC to the LRC. By 1907 the SWPEC, which had become known as the Scottish Section of the Labour Party, effectively ceased to exist. While this question hung in the air effective party organisation in Scotland could not take place.

This greatly perturbed Johnston, for whom a well-organised

Labour Party working closely with the trade unions was essential. Although he was often critical of the Labour Party at Westminster, Johnston regularly reaffirmed his belief in parliamentary methods. In 1910, as noted earlier, he was alarmed at the apparent drift from such methods. He chose at this juncture to set out clearly in *Forward* why he believed in the Labour Party as the road to socialism. In doing so he drew a response from the most significant Scottish Marxist of the day, John MacLean. MacLean was then a member of the Social Democratic Party (SDP, formerly the SDF). His Marxian dialectic and Johnston's socialist humanist polemic were joined in a fascinating debate.[22]

Johnston set out to uphold the value of the Labour Party against the apparent trend of opinion towards industrial unionism, and the 'purist socialist' approach of people such as Victor Grayson. Johnston claimed that the Labour Party's great strength was that it was democratic; it could genuinely claim to be the party *of* the working class as opposed to a party *for* it. Its relationship with the trade unions ensured that it was workers who financed the party, elected its officials and ultimately determined its policy. For Johnston it was therefore 'the heir of the Marxian tradition'. He went on to criticise as 'elitist' both the purism of such parties of the revolutionary left as the Socialist Labour Party (SLP), and the approach adopted by certain Fabians that socialism could be more quickly achieved by converting the top people in government and the establishment. In this he clearly followed Keir Hardie's type of 'middle road' socialism between Marxist dogma and Fabian permeation.[23]

Those who saw every concession to working-class welfare as 'palliatives', Johnston dismissed as peddling a theory of 'increasing misery'. Turning to the upsurge in industrial unionism, he welcomed the decline of the sectionalism of the craft unions, but argued that the tendency towards a federation of unions was not incompatible with workers' policical party:

In the slow process of evolving order from chaos, and the common-wealth from a mosaic of penury and plenty, I can see no reason why ideas not mutually exclusive should be placed in antagonism. The strike is still a weapon, so is political control, so is co-operative production, so is the boycott, so may be a million other things; to each their time and place as occasion arises. But the great broad principle of an association of wealth producers to capture political and economic control for the benefit of all is big enough to hold every section of us.

MacLean's reply latched on to Johnston's claim that the Labour Party was in the Marxian tradition. He accused the party of being a 'miserable caricature of Marxism'. For MacLean, the Labour Party was controlled by a 'reactionary Liberal element' which sought primarily to discredit the authentic Marxist approach of the SDP. MacLean believed that socialism could only be advanced by an amalgamation of the SDP and the ILP into a Marxist socialist party, free from the liberal-tainted policies of the Labour Party.

Johnston defended his claim by stressing that it was a Marxist axiom that the emancipation of the working class must be the work of that class itself. The Labour Party, he repeated, was a workers' party, and therefore the most appropriate vehicle for realising the Marxist precept. The SDP, on the other hand, was not associated formally with working-class organisations like the trade unions and the Co-operative Society. Instead of forming 'super parties', it was the task of socialists to turn the Labour Party into a socialist party: '"Socialists withdraw! Come out from among them and be ye clean!" may be an admirable sentiment, but it is a poor policy. Think you, if the socialists came out, it will leave the residue of Unionist working men, and Orangemen, and Liberal men, and "no politics" men, more class conscious, more rebellious, more intelligent, better educated?' For Johnston, there could be no socialist advance without the support of the masses. He accused MacLean of ignoring the organised section of the working class which was 'better educated', 'more class-conscious', and 'better fighting material'. MacLean, in Johnston's view, was instead sacrificing this advanced set of workers for those who were not even at the stage of seeing the benefits of trade unionism.

MacLean's main concern was whether or not the Labour Party was Marxist. In his view it was actually marching in an anti-socialist direction. MacLean did not dispute the necessity for a workers' party, but considered the Labour Party to be beyond the point where it could be such a party *and* socialist.

Johnston believed that the question of whether or not there should be a workers' party was the central one. In his view, MacLean in effect conceded the issue; arguments about how socialist this party was were secondary. He repeated that the character of the Labour Party would depend on how effectively the workers were educated. Without saying so in so many words, Johnston would appear to have been endorsing Ramsay Mac-Donald's notion that a party travelling in a socialist direction was preferable to one which was actually socialist.[24]

In the course of the debate Johnston made it clear that he rejected an approach which was totally based on the writings of one man. He admitted that he found Marx 'weary reading', and could not accept the determinism of Marxist doctrine. For Johnston, socialism required continual redefinition in the light of changes in society. In this belief he placed himself firmly in the strand of British socialism which emphasised individual agency and the spontaneity of change, and rejected the notion of socialism being imposed scientifically in accordance with a body of immutable laws.

The debate clearly illustrated the polarisation in the Labour movement in Scotland, as well as the rest of Britain, over the means of achieving socialism. Johnston had provided what he hoped would be seen as an inspiring vindication of gradualism free of any taint of complacency. It was a landmark in the context of arguments between British Socialists. Moreover, it gave a fillip to Labour Party organisations in Scotland which began to expand in the immediate pre-war years. The establishment of a Glasgow Labour Party in 1912 was of particular importance. The formation in 1911 of the British Socialist Party (BSP) which absorbed the SDP had the effect of further deepening the divisions on the Left. In response to the BSP, Johnston reproduced in *Forward* the original article in favour of a Labour Party which had precipitated the debate with MacLean. However, he also made attempts to maintain a spirit of free and open debate, and followed the *Forward* policy of giving space to all viewpoints.

Johnston's criticisms of industrial unionism during the Mac-Lean debate hardened into a more strident defence of the necessity of political action in 1911-12. This was in response to the emergence of the syndicalist movement. Syndicalism held that capitalism could be toppled by means of a general strike of the federated trade unions. The way would thus be left open for the seizure by the industrial working class, of the ownership and control of the tools of production. The movement was industrially and economically revolutionary; parliament and municipal councils were dismissed as all but irrelevant.

To Johnston such 'anti-politics' was folly. Moreover, it was not socialism; it was 'individualist anarchy'. Johnston argued that it was naive in the extreme to believe that workers who would not vote for a trade union leader in an election would obey his strike mandate. More importantly, syndicalists, in Johnston's view, did not grasp the implications of neglecting politics: 'With political power goes control of the army and navy, control of the judiciary, and control of the banks, that is: force, law and credit; and no class which deliberately hands over to its enemies the management and direction of these three weapons can hope for a successful issue of its economic struggles.' Johnston averred that syndicalists were leaving the capitalists 'entrenched in their strongest fortresses'.[25]

Johnston also believed that syndicalism's advocacy of craft – as opposed to state-ownership of different industries, would lead to a 'medieval guild system of production'. For Johnston, such an eventuality would mean individual greed and corruption on the part of the crafts, at the expense of the common collective good. There would always, in Johnston's opinion, be a need for the State to provide collective credit for different human enterprises; moreover, the State was necessary as the means of ensuring that the wealth created was used as a social product.

Johnston's stance led him into controversy with prominent Scottish syndicalists like William Gallacher, and into strong criticism of Tom Mann, the leading syndicalist figure in Britain. The corollary of this was an even closer identification with the approach of Ramsay MacDonald who, like Johnston, made better Labour party organisation his top priority. Johnston declaimed bravely and pertinently against syndicalism while making clear that he still believed in the efficacy of industrial action to bring about beneficial changes. However, in the eyes of the more zealous ILP activists for whom he had always been a fellow 'crusader', Johnston had become more orientated towards 'respectability' as a result of his interventions on the syndicalist issue. This was an image with which Johnston himself was by no means yet at ease.

V

The period 1912-14 saw Johnston continue to concentrate on his journalistic contribution to the Labour movement. *Forward*'s circulation probably topped 10,000 by this time. Johnston was an active Labour Party and ILP member but did not in these years seek nomination to office in either party. In the local political context, however, he was re-elected to the Kirkintilloch School Board in 1911, and elected to the Council itself at the end of 1913. An interesting career in municipal politics was about to unfold. In addition, he became the ILP representative on a Scottish Home Rule council, set up in 1912. Johnston was in favour of Scottish self-government, although he had led no meaningful campaign for it through the pages of *Forward*. The firmest endorsement he gave was a qualified welcome to the Young Scots Society, of which Roland Muirhead was a leading figure. In 1914 Johnston took time off political work to marry Margaret Freeland, who also hailed from Dunbartonshire, but from a somewhat more prosperous middle-class background.

Johnston also returned to the land issue in this period, with a series of articles in *Forward* entitled 'Who stole the Common Lands of Scotland?' The suffragettes continued to receive his support despite reservations over some of their militant tactics. The Glasgow Labour Party's policy of building cottages to be rented out at £8 to working-class families was just the type of municipal venture which appealed to Johnston's sense of the practical and the visionary combined. It was proposed to pay for the scheme out of the surplus in the city's tramway fund. Johnston picked holes in the liberal welfare reforms, in particular National Insurance, and refused to give the kind of endorsement offered by Sydney Webb.

This more combative radicalism of Johnston's came very much to the fore in response to the Dublin Lock-Out of 1913. He campaigned vigorously in the *Forward* on behalf of Jim Larkin, the Irish workers' leader, and started a fund for the striking workers' families. Johnston may have admired the political acumen of a Ramsay Macdonald, but he also saluted the passion of someone like Larkin. Indeed, his support for Larkin led him to criticise sharply those British Labour figures, such as Philip Snowden, whose opinion of Larkin and his tactics was less than enthusiastic. In the case of Dublin, Johnston believed Larkin had wielded the strike weapon as a last resort, and he dismissed charges of recklessness. Neither did he believe that Larkin was a syndicalist; 'he has too much hair on his head for that'. It was certainly true that Larkin did not repudiate parliamentary or municipal politics. However, his actions in practice in 1913 were clearly syndicalist in tendency, and he openly associated with outright syndicalists. This Johnston chose to ignore.

From early in 1912 Johnston had been turning his attentions to those firms which profited by war. 'We have long been of the opinion', he wrote, 'that if the Labour movement in this country wants to fight the periodic war scares effectively, it must be able to put its hand at once upon those who are reaping profit from the production and maintenance of munitions of war of all kinds.'[26] The Labour Party, Johnston argued, had to construct a policy of providing alternative work to that in 'war industries'. He suggested his favourite job-producing scheme: afforestation; and he advocated an eight-hour day on the railways which, he claimed, would mean employment for 100,000 more men, the slight dimunition of dividend being met by a reduction in taxation.

In August 1914 the 'periodic war scares' became a reality. The war industries boomed. Despairingly, Johnston wrote of how helpless the Labour movement was. *Forward* was going to the war.

2 A cool head on the Clyde (1914-1922)

Out of his intense anger, Johnston looked for a positive road through 'Armageddon'. With some prescience he wrote of the triumph of labour and democracy emerging from future reaction to the war.[1] However, he could not have foreseen just how momentous the events of the next few years were to be, both at home and abroad. Nor could his dread of the war have matched the appalling scale of the impending carnage.

Johnston primed *Forward* for a war of its own: against those he viewed as guilty of 'secret diplomacy', and against the 'home patriots' whom he accused of 'stabbing the working class in the rear'.[2] These became the targets of a column entitled 'Socialist War Points', a feature that was to add considerably to Johnston's reputation as a journalist and propagandist. It became a weekly scourge of war profiteers, and a consistent medium of anti-war argument. While other Labour leaders, such as James Connolly in Ireland, saw the war as an insurrectionary opportunity to upset capitalist governments throughout Europe, Johnston once again eschewed the barricades for the task of socialist education. For Johnston, the British people at least had willingly acquiesced in the war; Socialists and pacifists could only keep arguing their case.

The war effectively split the Labour movement in Britain. The ILP declared its opposition early on, although many of its members were either pro-war or believed that it had to be fought.

The Labour Party and Trade Union movement supported pro-secution of the war, chiefly because of the German invasion of Belgium. Those further to the Left were generally against – John MacLean most notably in Glasgow – although mavericks such as Victor Grayson (also of the BSP) and Robert Blatchford became positively jingoist and anti-German.

Johnston believed that secret diplomacy had been one of the main causes of the war. In a pamplet on the subject published shortly after the outbreak of war,[3] he accused the diplomats of being the tools of the 'ruling and financial classes', prepared to 'organise murder for fair interest upon investment'. The remedy, he argued, could only come when the people demanded demo-cratic control of the process of diplomacy. The Foreign Secretary, Sir Edward Grey, was roundly condemned by Johnston for 'secretly committing' Britain to war.[4]

Secret diplomacy was a siren cry too of Ramsay Macdonald. Macdonald resigned the chairmanship of the Parliamentary Labour Party on account of his opposition to the war, and went on to suffer the opprobrium of jingoist opinion for its duration. Macdonald's stance delighted Johnston, who considered his pre-vious defences of Macdonald in *Forward* thoroughly vindicated. Also lining up against the war was Johnston's other figure of inspiration, Keir Hardie. Johnston's sense of moral virtue, in such revered company, was palpable.

Forward, however, did not become a straightforward anti-war sheet. In keeping with his 'open-house' policy, Johnston allowed pro-war views to be expressed in the paper. On 5 September 1914, for example, there appeared an article by the Glasgow Labour MP George Barnes entitled 'Why Britain must win'. However, the most stridently argued pieces in favour of the prosecution of the war came from one of *Forward*'s resident scribes: Dr Stirling Robertson or 'Rob Roy'.

At first 'Rob Roy's' comments on the war had been full of

27

regret; he echoed Johnston's views on secret diplomacy, and condemned the circumstances which led to war. However, some six weeks into the war he came out squarely in support of the Allied cause and attacked 'German militarism'. From then on until the cessation of hostilities, 'Rob Roy' kept up a barrage of anti-German propaganda and identified the future of democratic socialism with the British Empire. With lofty eloquence he endorsed the notion of 'tribal duty' and the claims of nation over class. The pacifist stand of Johnston and the ILP was dismissed as indulgent: 'cloistered virtues won't serve the purpose, with the enemy thundering at the gates'.[5]

With *Forward*'s leading writer – next to Johnston himself – thus waving the flag, the impact of the anti-war case might have been blunted. In the event Johnston used the context of a developing debate with 'Rob Roy' to continually re-state it in fresh terms. Johnston was forced to make clear his position week by week, and if this led on occasion to tortuous reasoning, it was seldom less than lively and always honest. And it cannot be said – although some have –[6] that Johnston's views on the war changed significantly.

Johnston believed that Tsarist Russia was the most war-hungry of all the countries involved. He was not pro-German, and shared 'Rob Roy's' detestation of Prussian autocracy. However, he was hopeful that the Social Democrats in Germany would bring about revolution. This in turn could only happen if Germany were not threatened by Russian aggression. The prospects of socialism, in Johnston's view, were dependent on the destruction of militarism in every country: '. . . criticism of our military gang does not absolve the German military gang, but if we are always to run at the tail end of our Greys and Kitcheners, and the German socialists to run at the tail end of the Bernhardies and Hollwegs, goodbye to socialism'.[7] Johnston rejected 'Rob Roy's' tribal arguments, saying that the concern of working people should be defined in class terms. He added that the tribal justification logically committed people to fight in all wars, good or bad.[8]

These were Johnston's personal views, clearly stated. However, as editor of *Forward* he took care from the start of the war to keep the paper from infringing the Defence of the Realm Act. This meant in practice that anti-war viewpoints on sensitive topics such as recruiting could not be discussed lest they be interpreted as hampering the war effort. Similarly, the *Forward* made it a policy not to report or discuss industrial disputes in the war industries. This was to be of the utmost significance. Johnston was not in the business of making *Forward* a vehicle for heroic anti-war gestures. His first priority was to keep publishing the paper so that soberly argued propaganda against militarism would be heard.

Johnston did not, therefore, attempt to dissuade people from enlisting, unlike more high-profile socialist figures such as John MacLean. He stated bluntly that he did not believe in 'hissing the workers into a frenzied fury and taking to ourselves share of the aftermath of contrition and regret'.[9] This was interpreted by some, including 'Rob Roy', as 'shilly-shallying'. The latter was quick to make use of any ambiguity in the anti-war position. This seemed to be one in relation to Johnston, while the public pronouncements of Macdonald and Hardie supplied him with more substantial grounds for his accusations of confused thinking.

Macdonald in particular seemed to be trying to cover both his flanks. On 2 January 1915 *Forward* carried the following state-ment of his position: 'See the war through; establish democratic freedom and an unarmed peace in Europe; put an end to secret diplomacy; do justice to the families of the men at the front!' It thus appears that Macdonald's opposition to the war after it had started was heavily qualified; however, his misty rhetoric about peace and internationalism at ILP conferences fed a powerful myth which was to benefit his career after the war. Johnston did not lose faith in Macdonald – he later invited him to write a weekly column in *Forward* – but was quick to dissociate himself from the 'see it through' line of reasoning. In the same issue of *Forward* as MacDonald's statement, he wrote pointedly that the charge of 'shilly-shallying' could only be levelled at those who were anti-war in July 1914 and were now 'see it throughers'.[10]

As for Hardie, Johnston repudiated 'Rob Roy's' attempts to cast doubt on his stance by quoting at length a letter from Hardie on the subject of recruiting. The letter denied that he (Hardie) had ever supported any recruiting venture, or, equally, that he had tried to prevent young men from joining up. The letter continued:

> A Nation once in a war of such magnitude as the present, has no option but to press forward until suitable terms of peace can be reached. But it is for those who believed in the justice of the alleged cause which took us into the war, to convince our young manhood of the wisdom of enlisting. The policy of the ILP, as announced by the NAC, is one of complete neutrality, and to that I adhere.[11]

This was good enough for Johnston, and such a refusal to accept the necessity or the righteousness of the war was difficult for the censors to find fault with.

It was in such a vein that Johnston continued to write in relation to the war. He stressed that the righteousness of the conflict simply did not cease to be of account after the war had begun, whatever the dangers for socialism and democracy that a Germany victory would bring. To lose sight of the war's causes – in Johnston's view the conflict of rival capitalist interests and the secret machinations of diplomats – would be to write off the lessons he wanted the workers to learn. The opposition of socialists in every combative country was the only way Johnston saw of bringing the war to an abrupt end. On this point he and 'Rob Roy' filled more columns of debate, Johnston citing examples of Continental socialists defying their governments, 'Rob Roy' viewing them as hopeless aberrations against the tribal imperative. In 'War Points', Johnston exposed bogus stories of German atrocities, and publicised the ill-treatment being meted out to 'enemy aliens' in Britain. The ILP's opposition, he believed, would prove electorally wise in the long term.

On the other hand, Johnston was disgusted with the Labour Party. When Arthur Henderson joined the new coalition government in May 1915, Johnston feared for the future of the Party and for socialism in Britain. Labour, he believed, had thrown away its independence. He called for Macdonald and Snowden to lead the remnant of the Party in Parliament in the role of official opposition, and to campaign vigorously against the introduction of conscription. Unless they did this, the Labour Party, as Johnston viewed it, would be doomed. It was the height of frustration for Johnston to see the Labour Party, guided increasingly by a largely patriotic trade union movement, apparently lose its sense of radical spirit against a background of militarism and profiteering. As rents and food prices rose, the Labour Party was just another voice in a chorus demanding further sacrifices. However, for all his outbursts, Johnston could not bring himself to support an ILP breakaway from the Labour Party. As in the days of pre-war political and ideological ferment, Johnston saw no alternative to an organisation so based on working-class institutions.

The pressure towards a split was probably greater in Scotland, particularly Glasgow. Here the war had seen the initial patriotic jamboree simmer down in conjunction with rising social and industrial unrest. An engineering strike took place in several munitions factories in early 1915, foreshadowing a momentous conflict between skilled engineers and the Government later in the year. This was to be over the question of dilution of labour, that is the introduction of unskilled men and women into munitions work. Out of the former strike emerged the Clyde Workers' Committee (CWC), a group of militant shop stewards led by William Gallacher. Throughout 1915 a fierce struggle against rent increases and evictions developed in many areas of the city. *Forward* reported the rent strikes, though not the industrial disptues. Socialist rhetoric reverberated around Glasgow; the ILP and those to the left of it totally overshadowed the Labour Party; and the trade unionists, in contrast to their southern counterparts, fuelled the militancy. Some people were to get carried away with the scent of revolution, but Johnston's reflexes were more 'respectable'.

They were given full expression in *Forward* in reaction to a *Glasgow Herald* editorial which was concerned with the question of censorship measures against 'comparatively obscure journals' which addressed audiences not fit, in the Herald's view, to think or reason. Johnston presumed that *Forward* was considered one such journal, and was indignant. He replied that the paper was read by 'the intelligent people, the well-read, thinking, reflecting, clean-living, decent people'. He proudly boasted that gambling and sport were not covered by the paper, and that 'neither the bar-tender's pest nor the Sauchiehall Street dude ever spent a copper on a *Forward*'. People more comfortably off who had reached 'a certain level of culture' were the typical readers, because they could understand socialism and had the independence of character necessary to break with old traditions.[12]

On 26 September 1915 the personification of Johnston's values in such respects died. Keir Hardie was probably Johnston's only real political idol in the course of his career. As such he derived from him what served his ideals and ignored – or was perhaps genuinely unaware – of what did not.

In relation to what Johnston considered the essence of the Scottish character, Hardie was 'Scots to the very marrow ... introspective, logical-minded, but effusively kind, generously sympathetic and magnanimously charitable'. To Johnston Hardie had always been loyal to his class, however little the 'bar-tender's pest' might have appreciated it. Moreover, Hardie set, in Johnston's view, impeccable standards of personal conduct: 'He touted among Labour M.P.s for total abstinence pledges. A smutty story caused him to leave a railway carriage. He went nowhere to which he could not take his wife and daughter. He was, in the deepest, truest sense of the words, a christian gentleman'. Johnston wrote that Hardie had 'died of a broken heart', shattered by the cataclysm of war. He took consolation in Hardie's last words to him: 'When the people come to their senses again there will be a tidal sweep for Humanity.'[13]

II

Resistance to the Government's dilution schemes for the munitions industry escalated on Clydeside throughout 1915. Essentially, skilled craftsmen were seeking to preserve their jobs and status. Their fight was waged in uncompromising terms by both the Amalgamated Society of Engineers (ASE) in the interests of craft conservatism, and the shop steward's movement (the CWC was officially set up in October) for revolutionary socialism. The leading figure in the struggle who at this time seemed to accommodate both outlooks was David Kirkwood, shop steward at Beardmore's factory in Parkhead.

In accordance with his policy of publishing nothing which would lead to prosecution, Johnston kept *Forward* silent on the industrial disputes. This greatly annoyed the shop stewards and was to lead eventually to the CWC starting its own paper (*The Worker*) to put its case. Johnston was clearly wary of the shop stewards' movement on account of the syndicalist views of such people as Gallacher. According to the latter, Johnston looked kindly on the CWC only when it provided protection for pacifist meetings.[14] However, *Forward* did carry tentatively expressed criticism of the Government's Munitions Act of June 1915, perceiving it as advantageous to employers. Moreover, when it came to be expected that Lloyd George (Minister of Munitions) would visit Glasgow to smooth over the resistance to his dilution plans, Johnston commented: 'The Welsh Rarebit has not yet called on the Clyde Shop Stewards with his promised speech. Perhaps the visit had better be deferred till summer is a-cummin in, say about the 1st of April.'[15]

In the event Lloyd George duly turned up in Glasgow on 23 December and on this and the following day held talks with the shop stewards (including Kirkwood) at several munitions centres. During these talks Kirkwood and the other CWC leaders demanded workers' control of the industry as the 'quid pro quo' of dilution. This meant skilled workers' control over the number of semi-skilled and unskilled workers coming into the industry. Thus frustrated, Lloyd George decided to use a large meeting on Christmas Day to appeal over the heads of the shop stewards to the rank and file engineering workers in the cause of the nation's wartime needs. Instructions then went out from the Press bureau to newpapers that only the authorised version of Lloyd George's speech at the meeting should be published. It seems that Lloyd George hoped to create the impression that the shop stewards were unrepresentative extremists and that his dilution plans were found generally acceptable.

The meeting, as it turned out, was bedlam. Both Arthur Henderson and Lloyd George were denied a proper hearing, and only Kirkwood's appeal on behalf of the latter allowed him to make any kind of speech at all. Proceedings rapidly dissolved into knockabout rowdiness and Lloyd George was forced to call it a day amidst the disorder. Dutifully, however, the official press report carried his speech and conveyed the impression that only a small minority was hostile to the Munitions Act.

Forward had not received the Press Bureau's circular. As an 'anti-establishment' publication, it did not subscribe to the Press Association, and the latter was not disposed to send confidential instructions to it for that reason. However, as Johnston was to relate later, he knew all about the circular.[16] Nonetheless, he decided to go ahead and publish his own reporter's version of events. This included humourous interjections from the audience, and spared Lloyd George no embarrassment. Johnston prefaced the report by arguing that the censor's version should not be allowed to misrepresent the political significance of the meeting: 'It is simply stupid to go about deluding people that only an insignificant minority, and not the vast overwhelming majority of the meeting was angry . . .' On the other hand all references to military matters were left out, and Johnston again made it plain that he would publish nothing which he thought would bring the force of the authorities down upon him.[17]

The fact that he had not received the Press Bureau's circular gave Johnston a good alibi, and he was genuinely surprised when, on 3 January 1916, the *Forward* office was raided by the police. The offending issue of 1 January was suppressed, copies were rounded up, and *Forward* did not resume publication till 5 February. The decision to 'provisionally' suppress the paper had been taken on 31 December by a meeting of the Ministry of Munitions, attended by Lloyd George. Ironically, for all Johnston's pains to avoid such a development, his propaganda channel was temporarily closed.

The irony soon became apparent to those obliged to construct a case for the suppression. It had to be conceded that Johnston did not belong to 'the dangerous section of the Glasgow Socialists' and that *Forward* was not a seditious paper. The Assistant Secretary at the Ministry of Munitions, William Beveridge, had the utmost difficulty in drawing up a case under the Defence of the Realm regulations. Lloyd George, when called upon in Parliament to justify the suppression, had thus to resort to downright distortion.

Beveridge, indeed, compared his performance to 'trick cycling'. It consisted of using the fact that John MacLean's paper, the *Vanguard*, had also been suppressed to project its far more aggressive anti-war stance on to *Forward*; of twisting an attack in *Forward* on the Kaiser into one on the British monarchy; of baseless accusations that *Forward* itself seemed not to be in favour of freedom of the press. The only charge against *Forward* of any substance was that it had endorsed Kirkwood's demand for workers' control of the dilution process.[18]

Johnston answered some of the charges in a letter to the *Glasgow Herald* on 12 January, but his full defence did not appear until the reappearance of *Forward* on 5 February. This followed a meeting between Johnston and Lloyd George at which the latter insisted on three conditions before *Forward* could resume publication: (1) that it publish nothing prejudicing the military interest or safety of the country; (2) that it publish nothing interfering with the production or supply of munitions of war; and (3) that it publish nothing causing 'disaffection with the Munitions of War Acts or with the policy of the dilution of labour'.

Johnston had no difficulty in accepting the first two, for, as he rightly insisted, *Forward* had not offended in either sense before. The third prevented him from commenting – as he had done in the 1 January issue – on the dilution question. However, Johnston was too much of a pragmatist to baulk at this further constriction: 'It was that or nothing, and being Scots, we took that . . . we accept the inevitable on the principle that "Needs must when the Devil Drives". Short of the production of munitions, there is no interference with the right of political criticism.' He then went on to brief his readers and contributors regarding the 'rearguard action' nature of the paper's future defence of the working class. *Forward* would, he said, fight the introduction of conscription, but would 'retreat to the next line of defence' if it became an accomplished fact. Perhaps conscious that defeatism might have been read into such an attitude, Johnston urged his readers to 'keep shouting cheerily all the time for we are by no means a beaten rabble'; they were instead 'the children of the covenanters, in our veins beats the blood of Thomas Muir and the Chartist weavers and James Keir Hardie: our national anthem is "Scots What Hae"'.[19]

In such ways did Johnston draw on his pantheon of national radical heroes – 'Scots Wha hae' stood for Burns. The romantic in him vied with the pragmatist, but in the sense of the former's spirit embellishing the latter's deeds. The 'canny' Scot was in control of Johnston as he accepted Lloyd George's conditions. At all costs, in Johnston's scale of priorities, *Forward* had to publish; socialist views, however sanitised, had to find expression; and the effort to persuade the workers to the cause had to be rejoined – there was no sense in losing such a medium for a gesture which might turn out to be empty. Johnston, as has been noted, had no gambling instinct.

Neither did he have the temperament for prolonged confrontation with the Government. Johnston did not relish conflict with the law, and he was honest enough to make this clear. In addition, he may have been wary of the possible damage such a development could inflict: he spoke after all to the respectable working classes who had respect for institutions like the law. The upstanding and morally righteous image which Johnston tried to build around socialism owed much to an appeal to the democratic spirit enshrined in the distinctive Scottish legal and educational institutions. Johnston knew what he was aiming for, and, more important, what he was building on. In such a way the romantic linked up with the pragmatist. The latter, however, was in control.

The dilution struggle wore on into 1916 until the Government adopted heavy-handed tactics. At the end of March, Kirkwood

37

and five other shop stewards were arrested and deported. Johnston immediately set up a fund in *Forward* for them, and reported the episode as indignantly as the restrictions allowed. The Government was also helped by the fact that Kirkwood had split from the CWC, which was by this time indecisive and unsure of its ground.

The suppression of *Forward* has been viewed as part of the Government's strategy to defeat the CWC.[20] It is certainly true that the Government linked the *Forward* case with the general unrest on the Clyde. However, it is difficult to find evidence of a coherent strategy on the part of the Government in which *Forward* was used as a 'pawn'[21] Rather, as McLean has argued, it seems that the damage thought to have been done to the dilution scheme by the report of the Lloyd George meeting was what caused the Government to act.[22] The consequences, however, were embarrassing for the Government and beneficial for *Forward*: its sales and reputation rose. And it may be added that the paper's suppression had nothing to do with the subsequent confusion in the CWC; that was arguably the crystallisation of tensions between craft concerns and revolutionary impulses which had been present in the group from the start.

III

Johnston's abhorrence of the ravages of the war led him to denounce violence in response to matters nearer home. In June he wrote in *Forward* that: '. . . being socialists in the year 1916, we have had a surfeit of . . . violence; we have had it in Europe, we have had it in Dublin, and we have had it on the Clyde, and bluntly and briefly, we are "fed up" with it.[23] The tactics of the CWC and the militant left alienated Johnston. The language of bloody confrontation was foreign to him. He was astonished that James Connolly, someone with whom he had been in close contact through *Forward*, should have led the Easter Rising in Dublin.

Johnston looked upon Connolly as someone who was doing the necessary groundwork of socialist education like himself: a man who studied and wrote history, who polemicised vigorously, who grasped the possibilities of socialist theory and practice. Although Johnston acknowledged that Connolly's later writings had been 'more syndicalist and Sinn Fein nationalist' in character, he had yet believed that Connolly would be the last to be involved in what Johnston viewed as 'an obviously futile insurrection'. 'The psychology of it all', he wrote sorrowfully, 'is a mystery to me'. In fact, Johnston had published the evidence of Connolly's call to the barricades of the early days of the war, and he evidently chose to read little into Connolly's growing obsession with Irish nationalist mythology. Consistent at least with his strictures against violence, Johnston went on to condemn the executions of the rebels which followed.

little Orange bants.

Johnston was perturbed at the suggestion of violence surrounding 'direct action' beliefs. He responded by reaffirming his faith in the Labour Party and its ascent to power, this despite continuing criticism of the Party – and the movement generally – for not demanding nationalisation of the land and key industries as the price of their co-operation with the Government in wartime. For Johnston, direct action meant encouraging workers to do things for themselves through local government, trade union, Co-Operative and Friendly Society channels. He was all in favour of Workshop Committees and the training of workers for the control of their industries and their comunities. This was all consistent with and complementary to the political progress of the Labour Party; violence and revolutionary elitism were not. This outlook did not prevent Johnston giving support to John MacLean on the occasion of his wartime clashes with authority and subsequent prison sentences. However, *Forward* entertained a diminishing amount of 'direct action' propaganda – *The Worker* and *Vanguard* papers now catered for that – and strengthened its

39

Constitutionalist voice by having Ramsay Macdonald contribute a weekly column from November 1916. Both Macdonald and Johnston welcomed the February Revolution in Russia since they expected a social democratic outcome and anticipated movements towards a peace in Europe. They were to be disappointed in both cases.

Johnston's 'pacifism' was by no means absolute. This became clear early in 1917 when he dissented from the Bermondsey resolution which went before the ILP conference in April. This resolution stated that no Socialist should go to war whatever the reasons for the war. Johnston interpreted this as 'non-resistance to evil' and despaired of its impact on public opinion.[24] His view evoked a heated response, most notably from Willie Regan, a Glasgow ILP member who wrote the 'Catholic Socialist Society Notes' column in *Forward*. Regan rejected Johnston's interpretation of the resolution and argued that it simply pledged Socialists to refrain from going to war. It did not mean that husbands did not protect their wives from attack, or that workmen on strike were forbidden from forcing their way through a cordon of policemen to argue with blacklegs. Going to war, for Regan, was taking part in armed conflict in which people would be divested of initiative and would kill and invade on the command of those in power. Johnston, Regan charged, was arguing, in effect, for the continuation of armies and navies. Regan argued that winning votes was of little concern against principles.[25] Johnston replied by insisting on the need for international disarmament and support for such organisations as the League to Enforce Peace. The latter proposed that nations in dispute submit their quarrel to all the other nations in conference, not for a decision to be enforced, but merely for a report. Such a delay, in Johnston's view, would allow Socialists to organise working-class opposition to war.[26] By adopting the Bermondsey resolution, on the other hand, Johnston believed that the ILP would be opting out of political realities. He warned of the dire consequences for socialist advance. The conference, as it turned out, declined to take Johnston's advice and the resolution was carried. This certainly put Johnston at variance with most of his close ILP colleagues (although not MacDonald, who led the opposition), but it did not diminish his efforts on behalf of peace propaganda in the war taking place. Neither did it change Johnston's desire to see the ILP exert a strong influence over the Labour Party. He was critical of the block voting powers given to the Labour Party in the new constitutional provisions of late 1917, and feared that they would be used to 'smash the ILP'.[27] Johnston, indeed, was a member of the NAC of the ILP from 1916 to 1918.

Johnston's propaganda against war profiteering also continued apace. On the third anniversary of the war he brought out a pamphlet entitled *The Huns at Home During Three Years of the Great War*, which pulled together much of the material used in his 'War Points' column. It largely consisted of quotations from the 'Capitalist Press' which openly admitted the profiteering activities of high financiers, coal-owners and shipowners. And, for good measure, Johnston did not forget to include an account of the activities of the 'noble families'. It was, in sum, a devastating indictment out of the 'horses' mouths'. Johnston prefaced it as follows:

> Capitalism can have no notion of a commonweal; it can have no patriotism, since its very nature is to suck, leech-like, for profit irrespective of any national or social consideration, and a nation's hour of distress and extremity is capitalism's hour of greatest opportunity. During a war in which the nation is fighting for its life, capitalism will raise its rate of interest upon money loans; it will increase its shipping freight charges; it will raise its land rents; it will increase its charges for coal, iron and food; it will hold up supplies of vital commodities; it will, in short, exhibit itself even more nakedly than in times of peace, *as the real enemy of the people*.

ie. 'abnormal' Capitalism , but not capitalism per se ?

Thomas Johnston

Profiteering during the war seems to have sharpened Johnson's perception of class conflict. In a sharp exchange in *Forward* with George Barnes, Johnston scorned Barnes's attempts to play down class-consciousness in the interests of national unity. Johnston averred that 'capitalist class-consciousness' was in control of the state, that the profiteers were thus being protected by their class, and that Labour MPs in the Government were abandoning the struggle on behalf of the working class.[28]

For Johnston the capitalist class's concern for its own self-interest was never more in evidence than in its reaction to the Bolshevist revolution in Russia in October 1917. It was this which made him reluctant to condemn the anti-democratic actions of the Bolsheviks which attracted predictable fire from 'Rob Roy' by the end of 1917. For nearly a year Johnston was content to acknowledge that the Bolsheviks had made mistakes, but was more anxious to balance 'Rob Roy's' views in *Forward* and to accuse the capitalist press of reporting falsehoods.

Revolution in Germany at the close of the war gave Johnston hope that the Russian revolution would be saved for democratic socialism. He was optimistic that in Germany there would be no 'Spanish Inquisition or mass terror'. By this time Johnston was prepared to criticise openly the Bolsheviks' denial of political rights to the bourgeoisie. To Johnston such a move could only create a sense of injustice among the disenfranchised which was likely to hinder the successful development of the revolution: the bourgeoisie, after all, could only be elected by workers' votes and it was therefore a limitation on the freedom of the working class to decide their future. However, Johnston still believed that democracy as he liked to think of it might be established in Russia if the external threat of capitalist powers was removed.

It was truly a time of acute political ferment on the inter-national stage. The war had come to an end leaving devastation and much social and economic strife, but also heralding a climate of change and reconstruction. Johnston was genuinely hopeful that fear of the spread of bolshevism would temper the outcome of a 'capitalist–imperialist' peace in the interests of the working class in each European power.[29] He warned against punitive peace terms against the Germans, and hoped, above all, for international disarmament.

Domestically, Johnston prepared for the General Election. He had been persuaded to stand for the seat of West Stirlingshire which was adjacent to that of his native Dunbartonshire. It was a constituency with a significant mining community, and, given the portents of wartime unrest, looked ripe for a Labour swing. Johnston was a reluctant candidate because he knew there was a strong possibility of winning; he simply had no desire for a parliamentary career. Journalism and municipal politics constituted his happiest blend of activites. He had continued to be active in the latter arena throughout the war, and by the time of the election had also become a magistrate of Kirkintilloch. His municipal initiatives had already conferred on him legendary status at local level. He was responsible for establishing the first municipal picture house in Scotland, for the opening of a municipal cookery, for municipal fire insurance, for municipal baths and a bowling green, and municipal jam manufacture. As a member of the school board, both in Kirkintilloch and the wider Dunbartonshire county, he had been to the fore in the campaign to feed and clothe school children and to provide them with free school books. Election time also found him on the eve of finalising this scheme for Scotland's first municipal bank, which was duly set up in Kirkintilloch early in 1919. Back in 1917 Johnston had criticised Ramsay MacDonald for paying insufficient attention to municipal activity in his book *Socialism After the War*: 'Our Town and City Councils have as large, if not a far larger part to play in the building of the Socialist Commonwealth than have Imperial Governments, and we will make the cardinal mistake of our lives if we allow the opportunities which control of local government would give us, to slip past'.[30]

Johnston also made the land issue prominent in his campaign, calling again for nationalisation and afforestation schemes, and for the compulsory production of title. Johnston was still zealously committed to land reform and to the goal of forging an alliance between rural workers and small farmers and the Labour Party. To this end he was instrumental in securing an electoral alliance between the Highland Land League and the Labour Party. Johnston had also taken a leading part in the Scottish Home Rule Association (SHRA), set up by *Forward*'s benefactor, Roland Muirhead, in 1918. Johnston viewed Home Rule's potential benefits for socialism in the way he regarded municipal activity – opportunities for more people to feel involved in the running of their lives. He was not infatuated with it as a nationalist end in itself, and proclaimed that he 'would not cross the street to get a Home Rule that stopped at confining the exploitation of Scotsmen by Scotsmen . . .'[31]

The election proved extremely disappointing to Labour. They won only seven seats in Scotland, two of them ILP candidates. Johnston lost to the Coalition Conservative candidate by 6,893 votes to 3,809. His Liberal opponent, R. B. Cunninghame Graham, secured only 2,582 votes. The electoral alliance with the HLL turned out to be a failure. The situation in Britain as a whole was scarcely much better – Lloyd George's 'coupon' candidates were overwhelmingly returned in an atmosphere of 'Hang the Kaiser' recrimination. However, the election had been held under a defective register with inadequate voting arrangements for servicemen. The new franchise extensions of 1918 had still to take proper effect. The true reflection of Labour's growing popular strength was yet to come.

IV

Johnston used the opportunity of the post-election inquest to caution once more against loss of faith in political methods. In the 4 January 1919 issue of *Forward*, he laid out a potted history of working-class struggle in Scotland. This took as its starting-point Thomas Muir of Huntershill's 'Rights of Man' style of address in Johnston's native Kirkintilloch, and traced the story of political and industrial agitation through the radical weavers, the Chartists, and the early trade union movement up to Keir Hardie, the Scottish Labour Party and the ILP. The moral he drew from this historical odyssey was that the workers had oscillated from political to industrial action and back again, to the detriment of their potential capabilities. Such a 'see-saw' pattern had to stop in Johnston's view: both political and industrial weapons had to be used simultaneously. He was thus reiterating substantially the same arguments he had been using since the early days of syndicalist agitation. But he had never felt a greater need to make his point. The election results were, as Johnston realised, deceptive. Labour had polled over 323,000 votes in Scotland, its highest ever total by a long way. It had come painfully close to victory in several seats. As Johnston argued, the state of politics was one of flux; the Liberals had received a hammer blow at the election and the coalition could not go on indefinitely; realignment was in the offing. A favourable context seemed to be opening up for Labour in which only failure to improve organisation could deny it a vital breakthrough. Johnston stressed again his distrust of the 'sudden and catastrophic method of displacing capitalism' such as the mass strike, the Soviet or the seizure of workshops.[32]

However, the post-war climate also seemed conducive to such developments. The wartime industrial unrest had been as intense in several centres in England in 1917-18 as it had been on the

Clyde in 1915-16. Rent strikes had taken place throughout Britain in the course of the war. Social and economic expectations were unprecedentedly high after four years of rising living costs amidst the traumas of war. Lloyd George's populism could not rest solely on his claims to have won the war; he had also to promise the domestic rewards in the shape of houses, jobs and higher wages. Demobilisation in the early part of 1919 added to the social pressure which demanded successful and rapid reconstruction. The Government was not secure, its election victory notwithstanding, and it soon betrayed the fact.

In January 1919 engineering workers on Clydeside struck for a forty-hour week. Their demand was supported across the spectrum of the political Left, if not by other trade unions. The lack of support from the latter led to the adoption of picketing tactics and a rise in tension. On 31 January a mass meeting in Georges Square in Glasgow turned into a pitched battle between the police and large crowds of strikers and their supporters. 'Bloody Friday' resulted in a welter of cracked heads, and the arrest of Gallacher, Kirkwood and Emanuel Shinwell, then chairman of the Glasgow Trades Council, and three others. The day after the riot, troops were brought in and tanks rumbled along Glasgow streets. The strike ended in defeat. 'This is a strong Government', observed Johnston with bitter irony.[33] He was angry at the excessive response of the authorities, not least because he believed that it fomented a revolutionary fervour which would act as a distraction to the political labour movement in its most propitious hour. 'Direct action' appeals had seldom if ever found a readier response and the notion of a general strike gathered credence. Throughout 1919 the British participation in the war in Russia aroused widespread opposition among the British working class. 'Hands off Russia' became a genuinely popular slogan.

However, Johnston remained sceptical. He did not believe that a general strike would work: it was asking too much to expect the necessary mass of workers to be convinced of its necessity and workability. Furthermore, he challenged proponents of 'direct action' to clarify their case for it. In his view the only justification was as a measure to restore constitutional government in the event of a government doing the opposite of what it was elected to do. Direct action in these circumstances, Johnston argued, would compel a fresh election and would thus act as 'a constitutional check upon tyranny'.[34] And so Johnston's sterling defence of the ballot box against violence continued into 1920 against the 'Red Guardism' of his antagonists on the far Left, most of whom had now joined the newly formed Communist Party of Great Britain (CPGB).[35] The rhetoric of the revolutionaries, argued Johnston, had not reduced the death rate among the working class; that had been done by returning socialist municipal councils. He maintained that violence played into the hands of the Capitalists and 'drove our educative propaganda underground'.[36]

Johnston's most substantial single contribution to this propaganda task appeared in 1920. *The History of the Working Classes in Scotland* was a formidable piece of historical endeavour involving prodigious research and meticulous attention to detail. Johnston prided himself on having the skills of a historian, and expressed his desire frequently to take up the activity on a full time basis. First and foremost however, the book was a propaganda tool. As such the grim facts of the poor's historical lot took the form of a relentless indictment of a rather faceless parade of exploiters. However, a few cherished myths of Scottish history were also debunked on the way, including the romantic folk memory of the covenanters. This was curious given Johnston's recourse, at various times in his career, to the self-same myth.

The veteran socialist, William Stewart, was given the task of reviewing the book in *Forward*. He hailed it as 'The Book We Have been Waiting For', and as 'an historical act of great importance', and 'an achievement which must affect and help to shape future history'. This was not an exercise in sales hyperbole, at least not as end in itself. Stewart was expressing the typical Fabian/ILP faith in written propaganda as the main instrument of the ultimate socialist triumph. Johnston's belief that he was performing the most important task in the Labour movement was no egotistical conceit; it was shared by his peers. The usefulness or effectiveness of such propaganda was not questioned. It was simply assumed that once such a book got into a reader's hands it would have the desired effect. Stewart's only concern about the book's impact was the success of the distribution and publicity campaign for it.[37]

In his other chosen activity of importance – municipal politics – Johnston also made his most notable mark in 1920. This took the form of a municipal bank in Kirkintilloch. Under Johnston's guidance the Town Council (or ten members out of the twelve) formed itself into a limited liability company. The people were then given the inducement to invest in their own enterprise which offered three per cent interest on savings as opposed to the two and a half per cent of the other banks. The municipal bank then lent money to the town council at three and a half per cent interest as opposed to six per cent in the case of the capitalist banks. The scheme was a success both in the short and long term, and other Scottish burghs followed suit. To Johnston it was an example of 'practical politics' on behalf of the community as a whole. It was to be one of the achievements of which Johnston was most proud at the end of his political career.

By the beginning of the 1920s Labour's political progress in Scotland looked at once promising and uncertain. A mood conducive to radical change still obtained, if only in the shape of adverse public perception of the coalition Government's sluggish performance. Trade union membership had risen markedly during the war, and continued to increase steadily afterwards.

The ILP in Scotland recorded a membership peak in the year 1920-21,[38] but it slumped the year after. Moreover, the widening rifts on the Left between reformist and revolutionary perspectives threatened to damage the public credibility of socialism and labour politics generally. Similarly, in regard to the issues of the day, there seemed to be conflicting omens.

Unemployment and housing undoubtedly gave Labour grounds for optimism. The failure of the Government to provide jobs and proper housing despite promises and, in the case of housing, legislation, provoked widespread resentment. Such a failure was a gilt-edged opportunity for the Left to put the blame squarely on vested interests and monopolies, and to lead the reaction to the dismantling of the wartime economy which had at least extended the remit of the state in ostensibly collectivist directions. In a Scottish context, with the recurrence of rent strikes and protests in 1920, the housing issue provided an even greater chance for Labour to build up popular support. Both the ILP and Labour Party had worked closely with the rent strikers in 1915, and in 1920 they built on these community links to good effect. Labour's housing policies were constructive and cogent, and were communicated skilfully by John Wheatley on the Glasgow Council. Labour, in fact, waged something of a housing crusade during the war and afterwards. It made well-publicised protests in the Glasgow City Chamber, and drew attention to itself as the only party unfettered by landlord and financial interests, and therefore free to tackle the chronic problem at its roots. And chronic it certainly was: private house-building had virtually ceased before the war and no state provision followed afterwards despite promises to the contrary. In November 1920, after much compaigning on unemployment and housing, Labour won forty four seats on the Glasgow City Council. Glasgow, piped *Forward* joyfully if cannily, was 'Almost a Red City'.[39]

Yet the same *Forward* reports of these elections revealed the continuing significance of the issue which had always plagued Labour: religious sectarianism. In the course of a ward-by-ward assessment of the elections, Willie Regan of the Catholic Socialist Society instanced cases of Labour being damaged by rival Orange and Green candidates and sectarian appeals to voters. He concluded: 'The working class are evolving gradually towards Labour and are at different stages of development. Many partial converts have unfortunately diluted their Labour support with national prejudice . . . '.

As in the pre-war period the issue drew much of its force from events in Ireland. By 1920 that country was in turmoil, with open war in the south between the British Army and the Irish Republican Army (IRA), and sectarian rioting in the north between Protestant and Catholic workers. Sinn Fein's republican separatism had, in the aftermath of the Easter Rising reprisals, eclipsed the Home Rule movement in Ireland. In Scotland, this development was to a large extent echoed among the Irish communty. This was at first viewed with dismay by Regan and the Catholic Socialist Society, and also by Johnston. However, British military repression, in the form of the 'Black and Tan' excesses, drove the Labour movement to the cause of Irish self-determination, even if this did mean Sinn Fein's vaunted Republic. The ILP and the Labour Party in Scotland held 'Hands off Ireland' rallies at which straightforward Irish Nationalist sentiment all but drowned out socialist argument.

This was a risky political game to play. Protestant working-class voters, whether of the Orange variety or not, might be alienated. Moreover, there was no certainty that Irish Catholic voters were going to come to Labour in great numbers, whatever the encouraging signs. Johnston was sensitive to these risks. In the 14 May 1921 issue of *Forward*, in the wake of an IRA shoot-out in Glasgow which left a policeman dead, he expressed his fears that Labour would suffer as a result. He thought the incident would be likely to lead to a backlash among Scottish Protestant workers, just as the latter were becoming sympathetic to the plight of the Irish people under the 'Black and Tans'. The one real hope for Ireland', he wrote, 'is the growth and victory of a working class party in this country pledged to yield Self-Determination to Ireland.' The shooting of a policeman, in his view, made this task all the harder.

Johnston's concern to balance Labour's appeal to both Protestant and Catholic workers should be seen in the context of the changing political circumstances of the period. In 1918 Labour had made a blatant bid for the Catholic vote by shelving its secular educational principles. The Education Act of that year brought Catholic schools into the State system on an equal financial footing to non-denominational schools. Labour presented itself as the party prepared to defend the interests of Catholic schools on the Education boards, and the Catholic Church, notwithstanding its fears of the spread of socialism, came to value that support. Along with Labour's more radical stance in the Irish issue, such a development seemed to remove the most formidable obstacles to Irish Catholic votes. Astute political organisers in the Glasgow ILP such as Regan and Patrick Dollan now moved to inherit the electoral 'machine' of the United Irish League. Dollan also attempted to douse Labour's prohibitionist tendences, and to alter its 'Calvinist' attitudes to leisure and recreation generally.[40] In the November 1920 municipal contests, there was a marked shift to Labour in most Irish Catholic wards, despite the persistence of sectarian squabbling.

Johnston remained strongly prohibitionist, more than a little Calvinist and very conscious of working-class Protestant votes. He still thought that Labour's natural base of support was the native skilled artisans. He was probably more cognisant of the strength of the Ulster Protestant resistance to Irish nationalism than many of his colleagues, although he did not accept their case. In general he shared most of the British Labour movement's simplistic assumptions about the Irish question and made no real attempt to assess the implications of an Irish nationalist state for socialist politics and the working-class interest. However, when the British Government opened peace negotiations on the issue in the summer of 1921, Johnston praised the initiative.[41] Wheatley, among others, criticised him for appearing to give a blessing to partition. Johnston denied he was doing this but remained supportive of the British Government's attempts to end the deadlock. Significantly, he raised no objection to the eventual Anglo-Irish Treaty of December 1921 which duly formalised partition, albeit ambiguously. Attempts to woo Orangemen to Labour, which were at least semi-serious, were also made by Johnston in *Forward* in this period. As it was the Anglo-Irish Treaty effectively removed the Irish question from British politics while providing for its escalation into civil war in Ireland itself.

In spite of his interventions on the matter, Johnston had no real affinity with the 'Billy and Dan' aspect of urban Scottish political culture. He recognised its importance to Labour's fortunes, but lacked the insight of people such as Dollan who were, by background and instinct, closer to it. Johnston had too woolly a concept of how to overcome sectarian divisions, and often resorted to an Olympian type of response. He was much happier at this time attempting to prevent the ruin, as he saw it, of rural Scotland, or arguing for a reduction in the rate of interest on the National Debt. In relation to the former, Johnston believed that Labour lacked a coherent agricultural policy: he called for a programme of soil cultivation and the resettlement of people on the land. The topic of the National Debt brought Johnston into conflict with Sidney Webb who cautioned against his advocacy of a reduction in the war loan interest.

Controversy over such issues reflected the degree to which the political stakes had risen. An election loomed and strategic calculation about voters and issues had never been so vital to the Labour Party. It was now looking increasingly like a genuine contender for power. Johnston himself was standing again in West Stirlingshire.

The election took place in November 1922. It resulted in an historic breakthrough for Labour in Scotland, especially in urban industrial areas: twenty-nine seats were won, ten of them in Glasgow (out of fifteen). Johnston triumphed by 895 votes in a straight fight with the Conservative incumbent. Of the Clydeside MPs (including Johnston) almost all were ILP nominees. In Britain as a whole Labour won 142 seats and became the second largest party in Parliament.

On the eve of the election Labour in Scotland had benefited greatly from a test case over the rent issue which resulted in victory for the tenant (Bryde) against the factor (Kerr). Bryde's case had been funded and fought by the Glasgow Labour Housing Association, and the victory was a culmination of Labour's efforts on behalf of a popular struggle. Moreover, only Labour held out the promise of ensuring that the gains made were not reversed in subsequent legislation. Johnston had no doubts about the rent case's importance in his analysis of Labour's successes; ' . . . the Rent Act decision in the midst of an election campaign was a gift from the gods; and the Irish Treaty has cut the ground from underneath the feet of the politicians who lived by cultivating Billy and Dan wars in the ranks of the working class'.

After tumultuous years of strikes and riots at home and wars and revolutions elsewhere, Labour had got the kind of response from the people which to Johnston meant real progress. Faith in parliamentary means of social change had been restored. Johnston viewed it as vindication of propaganda and the stamina of the 'educators'.

The mood was one of genuine popular euphoria. The hopes of thousands of workers found evangelical expression in an emotional send-off for the Clydeside MPs at St Enoch's station in Glasgow. Both the 'Red Flag' and popular psalms were sung. The train to London departed choked with declarations of intent and promises of better times.

Johnston's reflections on the elections correctly stressed the rent issue and the effects of the Irish Treaty. Memories of the 1915 Rent Strikes were still vivid; the fight waged then was to a large extent continued into the 1920s. Successive pieces of legislation on the issue improved the position of the tenants but each had its limits, and the traumas of eviction continued to be visited upon working-class families. Labour's identification with the struggle was total but it did not dragoon the people involved. Rather, the open style of organisation of the ILP in particular encouraged wide working-class participation.[42] Just as Johnston's refusal to turn *Forward* into a doctrinaire 'hot house sheet' arguably attracted an increasing number of new readers, so the ILP's tactics got hitherto non-political people involved in a popular movement. The revolutionary Left never really started to build up such a popular base.

The rent struggle and the demand for better housing provision were priority issues which crossed ethnic and religious divisions and got support for Labour from both Protestant and Catholic workers. Indeed, the vast majority of those involved in the rent strikes were Protestant skilled workers and their families, some of whom were Orange Order stalwarts.[43] It was not an uncommon sight in 1915 to see protest banners alongside Union Jacks in tenement closes, and the use of the archetypal Protestant Ulster slogan of 'No Surrender' was perhaps not entirely coincidental.

The Irish issue's removal from British politics meant that the Catholic working class became more politically preoccupied with their own deleterious social and economic conditions. Catholics and Labour found that they needed each other. In addition, Labour was now free to direct its appeal to the Protestant working class on these issues without the risks which a high profile Irish campaign ran.

Labour could only have made such an electoral breakthrough in 1922 with the support of the Irish Catholic 'machine', and large numbers of Protestant workers, skilled and unskilled. It achieved this support because of its policies on certain issues and its improved organisation; and in spite of the persistence of sectarianism and deep ethnic consciousness. It was also helped considerably by a growth of class-consciousness, arguably moulded by the phenomenon of the 'Red Clyde'. It has been argued, rightly, that the rent and dilution struggles were not of themselves revolutionary.[44] However, the *cumulative* effect on the working class of the successive struggles, protests, arrests and deportations, and government repression was arguably profound. The public became more aware of socialist leaders and their politics. Trade unions for the first time played a role at government level. People began to believe that it might be in their power to effect change.[45] This was a revolution of a kind and it was a revolution which led to an increased sense of class identity across skilled and unskilled divisions, and orientated more workers towards Labour politics.

How big a part did Johnston play in this? The answer must lie in the impact of his propaganda and his attempts to 'educate' his readers. This is impossible to measure with any certainty. However, it can be stated firstly that his work was reaching an increasing number of people. *Forward*'s circulation rose every year from 1914, particularly after its suppression.[46] In his Directors' Report of 1917, Johnston wrote: 'The status and influence of the *Forward* has vastly increased, and it is being regularly quoted by the democratic press all over the world.' The pamphlets produced by the *Forward* printing company had all sold out by 1917. *The History of the Scottish working Classes* was said to have broken sales records for a book of its price and format. Johnston's column

'Socialist War Points' was much admired and referred to in British Labour circles.[47] And perhaps the most telling indication of Johnston's standing as a journalist came in a London anti-Labour journal *The Truth Teller* in 1920. This journal paid Johnston the compliment of worrying about his 'cleverly destructive' propaganda, and admitted that 'he has as neat a punch as any writer in the business'.[48]

If the First World War led to popular disaffection with the governing classes, and the exposure of folly and corruption in ruling circles,[49] then Johnston must be credited with helping to shape this popular mood. He kept up a weekly barrage of such disclosures and pursued the ruling class with a withering scorn. Johnston's readability and entertainment content probably facilitated the attainment of his most serious objectives. Similarly, his relentless attack on war profiteers lost nothing in their use of irony and subtlety. More than anyone else, Johnston made this issue his own, and undoubtedly tapped a rich seam of popular anger. The *Huns at Home* may not be his most renowned publication, but it was probably the one which spoke loudest to the working class in the context of its time. Johnston was a crucial influence in building up a clamorous sense of injustice among the Scottish working class. There was something that bit more substantial about the cumulative effect of his writings in *Forward* and elsewhere than the ephemeral if rousing oratory of the more flamboyant and messianic Labour and socialist spokesmen of the day.

During the war the maintenance of *Forward* was Johnston's first priority. Stirring anti-war speeches which led to arrests and jail sentences were not his way of responding to the challenges of the time. He did not in any way disparage the sacrifices of people such as John MacLean in this respect. However, he found the value of such actions questionable:

He (MacLean) is paying the price. He advocated a Social Revolution by Bolshevist methods, and, alas, the bulk of the workers do not want a Social Revolution by any method, but go on in rivet-hammering competition and scrambling for overtime, and regard the John MacLeans as 'decent enough but a bit off'. The blood of the martyrs is said to have been the seed of the Church, and John MacLean's dramatic sacrifice may do more to shake up the brains of the working class than did John MacLean's years of educative propaganda for socialism, but it is only upon such a presumption that the sacrifice can in socialist tactics, be justified.[50]

Johnston did not share the presumption. He saw no shortcut to the radicalisation of the working class. He believed that heroic self-sacrifice would be out of proportion to its impact on the mass of the people. He thus had no desire to make of *Forward* a *cause célèbre*. There were, in his view, more important tasks for it to accomplish: socialist arguments and ideas had to be kept in circulation, an anchor of reason and cogent propaganda had to be provided in a climate of excess and folly. He had, by the end of 1922, the election triumph to point to in justification of his stance. The benefits of his pragmatism for the working class might thus be seen to have outweighed any loss of 'honour' entailed in his willingness to compromise.

However, it might also be contended that the value Johnston placed on propaganda and education prevented him from grasping properly the importance of other developments in relation to the working class. These largely concerned the unskilled and in particular the Catholic workers. Johnston's disavowal of *Forward* being read in the slums has been noted. The assumption inherent in it was that the poorest workers would not rally to Labour in the circumstances they were then in. By the 1920s the evidence against this was plain for Johnston to see. The work of his colleagues, Dollan and Regan, had made Labour voters out of people relatively uninfluenced by Labour propaganda. They had done so by means of social and religious contacts, personal communicability and astute 'brokerage'. They cut with the grain of popular culture to establish new and durable voting habits.

For many of the unskilled, Protestant and Catholic, the ability to vote was very new indeed. It arrived only in 1918. Despite, therefore, the neglect of Johnston and *Forward*, many of these workers identified from the start with Labour. In the case of such workers, the growth of trade unionism among their number provided the medium through which political awareness was fashioned. The trade unions now played a part in such workers' lives which could translate day-to-day experience into a firm sense of political identity. Equally, many people were simply turning towards Labour for their own personal reasons based on their own experiences.

Johnston made no real acknowledgement of such developments. He thought too loftily of socialist politics as the medium of well-read, thinking people' decisions, when it was for many an identification based on personal foible, social pressure or ambiguous reasoning which owed nothing to socialist propaganda. Labour was not above the complex and murky political world as Johnston's ethically flavoured style could sometimes suggest.

But his contribution to Labour's advance in Scotland was nonetheless as powerful in its way as that of the movement's more colourful or more populist leaders. Propaganda clearly did have its role to play. Johnston was the antithesis of the 'Red Clydeside' legend, yet he played no small part in its creation. In a politically heated era his was a cool head which never lost its way.

3 Labour and the Empire (1922-1929)

The new Clydeside MPs travelled to London consumed with missionary zeal. Fired by their send-off, they descended upon Westminster determined not to be diverted from their socialist objectives. They were openly scornful of parliamentary etiquette. In his maiden speech, Johnston was as strident as any of the rest in his declaration of intent:

> Some of our (Scottish Labour) speakers, perhaps, have not addressed the House in the polished accents of Oxford or Cambridge. We do not pretend to come here to throw about Latin maxims, to utter any pleasantries, or to offer meaningless courtesies, for most of them are meaningless. We have come here to ask reasonably and courteously that the Government should face the fact that the common people of our native land are in a state of starvation. You are in a majority. You refuse our remedies. What are you going to do?[1]

Johnston fully shared in the sense of urgency which distinguished the new group of MPs. They believed they could highlight the problems of poverty and social inequality in the tradition of their guiding spirit, Keir Hardie. They thought they could shame the Government and, indeed, Parliament by relentless exposure of injustice. Unemployment was the obvious target for such an assault, and Johnston was quick to express to the House the conviction that it could ony be remedied by increasing the purchasing power of the working class. He argued that a major factor in weakening that purchasing power was the continuing burden of the War Debt and the interest on it, a burden borne disproportionately by the workers. Such economic arguments set the tone of his critiques for the coming years.

He subscribed at an early stage, therefore, to an under-consumptionist school of economic thinking which owed much to the writing of J A Hobson. In this respect he developed his critiques of the existing economic order in tandem with John Wheatley. From late in 1922 until around the middle of 1925 Johnston and Wheatley were to provide the economic thought of the Scottish Labour contingent at Westminster in a way in which each man complemented the other. This was also true of written propaganda: Johnston kept up a barrage of arguments in *Forward*, developing economic themes he had been picking over since the war; while Wheatley published his ideas on unemployment and wealth distribution in an influential pamphlet, *Starving in the Midst of Plenty*. The two men stressed the themes of under-consumption at home *and* abroad; the undercutting of domestic industry by foreign competitors who used sweated labour; trading within the Empire; and the Empire as an instrument of socialist progress. Such themes, as will be explained, led to important debates within the Labour movement. They also led Johnston into a deep and controversial association with colonial affairs.

Wheatley was a more intellectual figure than Johnston. His thinking in this period – as in earlier years – has some claim to originality. Johnston, however, was adept at refining ideas; his journalistic skills gave him an instinct for cogent emphasis or clearer reformulation. Moreover, Johnston could quite profitably develop ideas into wider-ranging arguments which made connections between themes and teased out the practical implications of theories which were often tortuous. Both Wheatley and Johnston, if Johnston less obviously, took impressive intellectual charge of the breakthrough achieved by Labour in Scotland in 1922. Both sensed an important opportunity to prime the Labour Party for Government in an intellectually substantial and robust fashion. In personal terms, however, they were somewhat distant from one another. Johnston was not of the Clydeside group in the way that Wheatley, Maxton, Kirkwood, Stephen and Buchanan were. Wheatley was closest to Maxton who, in terms of charisma, overshadowed the rest.

The Clydesiders featured in several rumpuses during their first parliamentary session. The one most publicised concerned Maxton's 'murderer' charge in relation to Sir Frederick Banbury, a Tory MP who spoke in favour of a reduction in the Scottish Health Estimates. Maxton had recently lost his wife, whose death had been the result of the strain involved in tending to the illness of their young son. Maxton was suspended for using – and refusing to withdraw – 'unparliamentary' language, and Wheatley, Buchanan and Stephen, by repeating his charge, incurred the same penalty. Johnston, too, was supportive, and defended Maxton in *Forward*. Indeed, Johnston courted libel actions by his assertion that 'every MP who was art and part in the shameful decision to cut the milk grants to the Local Authorities, and thereby caused the deaths of children, is himself in fact and indeed a murderer'.[2] Johnston, by now on the executive of the Parliamentary Labour Party, still stressed the need for an active, campaigning ILP, and firmly rejected the notion that the Labour Party should avoid upsetting middle-class voters.

But Johnston's preferred method of making his presence felt was to adapt to the House of Commons his journalistic style of exposing financial or business malpractice. As such, in December 1922, he raised the issue of a public grant of £3½ million which the Government had guaranteed to a commercial company operating in the Sudan. Johnston revealed that the Liberal leader Herbert Asquith had headed a deputation to the Government to lobby for the grant, and that Asquith's son was a director of the company in question. Johnston claimed that he was primarily concerned to attack the practice of giving public money to enterprises which were making substantial dividends. However, the thinly veiled insinuation that Asquith had acted out of personal interest was, predictably, the cause of a furore which embarrassed the Labour leadership. Johnston was warned at the time by the Party Whip that his career would suffer if he did not withdraw. Johnston refused, and had to listen to an emollient speech by MacDonald in which the latter dissociated himself from Johnston's suggestions.

Johnston was in fact torn between his desire to propagandise vigorously from the parliamentary stage, and his sympathy for MacDonald's difficulties as party leader. Despite his lukewarm embrace of a parliamentary career – and his continuing preference for journalism – Johnston rapidly became an effective House of Commons performer. A contemporary wrote of him: 'His forceful debating style, his assiduity in the collection of information on the subjects with which he dealt, his somewhat sardonic humour, made him as effective in the House of Commons as he was in the columns of *Forward*.'[3] Johnston prepared his contributions thoroughly and presented his arguments persuasively. He disliked London and was contemptuous of social 'junketing' – as were the other Scottish Labour members. Several critical pieces appeared in *Forward* on this topic in the early 1920s, with Johnston at his most acerbic. This was another example of his – and the Clydesiders' – determination not to be side-tracked by frivolity. However, such contempt for parliamentary and social conventions angered MacDonald, and Johnston was sensitive to the latter's pleas for party unity. Johnston, and the Scottish contingent in general, with the possible exception of Maxton, backed MacDonald as Parliamentary Party leader. Johnston at least believed that there was thus a sense of obligation to assist Mac-

Donald in making Labour appear fit to govern. Johnston was certainly less reckless or gratuitously disruptive in his parliamentary behaviour than, for example, Kirkwood, Maxton or Stephen. But, in 1922-23, the unity of the Clydeside group was nonetheless more apparent than that of the Parliamentary Labour Party as a whole. The MacDonald approach was clearly at odds with that of the ILP, typified by the Clydesiders. Johnston straddled the divide between them while – for the moment – taking greater political risks on behalf of the 'pilgrims of St Enoch'.

The Clydesiders barely had a chance to enjoy their notoriety before another election was sprung on the country. Conservative Prime Minister Stanley Baldwin decided, in November 1923, to adopt protection as party policy, and duly sought a popular mandate. For Johnston, the resurrection of the Free Trade–Protection debate was a 'mock struggle' distracting attention from the priority issue of under-consumption. It was to this issue that the ILP's *Socialist Programme* – published at this time – largely addressed itself, and Johnston urged the Labour Party to follow suit. Johnston, like other ILP leading figures of the time such as H. N. Brailsford (also an accomplished socialist journalist) and Clifford Allen, was becoming increasingly concerned with the economic and monetary theory bound up with the problem of unemployment. Johnston also fed arguments about sweated labour into the unemployment debate; he believed that this was an issue that Labour could use against both the Tories and the Liberals. Johnston cited the Tories' opposition to a bill fixing minimum rates of wages for every industry as evidence of their willingness to accept low wages and sweating in British industries. With wage cuts, of course, went a decrease in purchasing power and hence unemployment. In relation to the Liberals, Johnston argued that they would not be prepared to prohibit the importation of sweated goods from abroad. Johnston contended that the raising of living standards was not compatible with a free market for sweated goods whether produced at home or abroad.[4] This was a theme he was to return to in relation to Imperial questions.

Baldwin's recourse to the ballot box did not give him the result he wanted. The Tories emerged as the largest party (258 seats), but without an overall majority. Labour won 191 seats, ahead of the Liberals on 159. The Liberals quite obviously would not support a protectionist Tory government in office. In Glasgow and the West of Scotland Labour improved still further on the 1922 showing. Johnston himself increased his majority in West Stirlingshire to over 3,000.

The Clydesiders were unanimous in their advice to MacDonald after the election. In *Forward* Johnston, Wheatley and Maxton called on him to return to the country for a mandate to govern. Johnston thought that such an appeal should be made mainly on the basis of measures to fight unemployment, although he was also keen that Labour should promise to refuse cabinet salaries and pensions. When it became clear that MacDonald was going to form a minority government, Johnston looked forward to it being 'beaten gloriously', such a defeat being the condition for a decisive victory and the acquisition of real power. Johnston's confidence in such an outcome seemed unshakeable.

When MacDonald had formed his team, only Wheatley, as Minister of Health, represented the Clydesiders. The claims of Johnston and Maxton had been passed over. Johnston was disappointed, although he could not have been greatly surprised, given the bad taste left by the Sudan episode. Johnston would have welcomed an appointment to the Scottish Office – either as Secretary or Under-Secretary – to tackle issues dear to his heart such as the redevelopment of rural Scotland, the fishing industry in Scotland, and the conversion of deer forests to small holdings. These were all issues which had occupied him in his early days as an MP. MacDonald might have been well advised to accommodate Johnston. By keeping him out MacDonald only sharpened Johnston's critical faculties.

II

From the time of his election to Westminster Johnston had found the demands of being an MP and and a newspaper editor something of a strain. Consequently, in January 1924, he appointed an acting editor, Emrys Hughes. Hughes was a young Welshman who had already made his mark in the field of socialist journalism and propaganda. He was greatly influenced by Keir Hardie and was later to marry his daughter. Like Johnston he placed overriding emphasis on the role of propaganda in the socialist cause. Moreover, he was also a teetotaller and an admirer of Robert Burns. Clearly the character of *Forward* was safe in Hughes's hands.

Hughes first met Johnston in *Forward*'s cramped office near St Enoch's square in Glasgow. His description of Johnston captures well the imposing, esoteric and idiosyncratic aspects of the latter's physical presence: 'He had a shrewd, rather gloomy lined face which reminded me a little of the portrait I had seen of Carlyle in his early years, grim, stern, rather fanatical until he smiled. He wore a Gladstonian collar and a blue spotted bow tie and was smoking a big pipe.'[5]

Johnston thus eased his editorial burden, but he continued to contribute his weekly front-page column, 'Socialist War Points', and regular articles on a range of topics. Whenever he felt that the Government deserved criticism, he did not hesitate to deliver it, both in the pages of *Forward* and in the House of Commons. Once again, he made an issue out of Labour MPs moving in 'High Society' and wearing court dress, while on the subject of unemployment, Johnston accused the Government of procrastination. 'Men who sit and stare at their navels for months on end', he wrote acidly in *Forward*, 'may be suited to Thibeten temples, but not to the control of British Departments of State.'[6]

Perhaps more significantly, he did not allow the Sudan issue to rest. He harassed the Under-Secretary for Foreign Affairs, Arthur Ponsonby, about the matter, asking embarrassing questions about the control of the company's profits, the economics of the cotton-growing scheme which the company ran, and the exploitation of labour. The Labour Government, to Johnston's disgruntle-ment, did not propose to revoke the guarantee of £3½ million to the company. When the issue came to be decided, Johnston – along with thirty-six others on the Labour side – voted against the Government, which drew much of its support from other quarters.

The Sudan issue reflected Johnston's deepening immersion in colonial affairs. During the time of the first Labour Government he became recognised as one of the Party's foremost spokesmen in this area, notwithstanding his criticism of some of the Party's positions. During 1924 he was also largely responsible for initiat-ing and directing the debate within the Labour movement on socialism and the Empire.

Through his study of colonial questions such as the Sudan, Johnston came to develop a positive concept of Empire. Johnston came out against Britain handing over the Sudan to Egypt. Such a development, he believed, courted the risks of Egypt returning the Sudan to the status of a slave plantation. In view of Egypt's refusal to accept League of Nations control of Sudan, Johnston argued that Britain had no option but to stay. He was immediately assailed by many on the Left – particularly Communists – accusing him of supporting British Imperialism.

To this Johnston replied with an appeal to Socialists to reassess their view of Empire. He argued that socialism would not be advanced by the disintegration of Empire; indeed, this would mean 'fresh wars and reconquests, wholesale decimations, fire, slaughter, and a relapse to barbarism'. Johnston characterised socialist anti-Imperialism as a latter-day form of 'Whiggery' – a

Cobdenite ideological leftover which was no longer relevant. He pointed to the existence of Labour governments in Australia and other Dominions, and saw in them an obvious basis for greater unity and international co-operation. In the light of such developments, Johnston held that Socialists should shun 'the stale and fly-blown phylacteries of a discredited anti-socialist Whiggery'. Johnston envisioned, under socialist guidance, an Empire with Home Rule all round and a federated parliament dealing with the affairs of common concern. In this way, he concluded, the Empire 'might be made the greatest lever for human emancipation the world has ever known'.[7]

In accordance with these views Johnston urged the Labour Government to evolve trade policy in relation to the Labour governments of the Dominions. To Johnston, the economic possibilities were enormous: Britain could engage in collective purchasing and marketing of Empire foodstuffs and raw materials; there could be bulk exchange of surpluses between Britain and the Empire countries; co-operative schemes in marketing and distribution could be established; the Empire could function as an economic unit to the detriment of middlemen and speculators. In Johnston's view, Labour had the chance to develop a policy of Imperial preference from a socialist standpoint: namely, as a means of stopping the importation of sweated goods. Trading with Dominions in which Labour governments outlawed sweating, was to Johnston far preferable to trading with countries which allowed sweating to take place. He said in the House of Commons: 'I submit that it is our business as a Socialist Party and a Labour Government to examine the origin of our imports if we are going to be a Labour Government at all.'[8]

There were other Labour MPs who fully agreed wth Johnston. With a small group of them – including George Lansbury – Johnston set up a Commonwealth Labour group to promote the Empire with such socialist reasoning. Estimates of the group's numerical strength and its overall impact on the party vary. However, even if its activists never numbered more than twenty or thirty, the group did succeed in forcing such issues on to the Labour Party agenda. They managed to get resolutions debated and passed at party conferences, and, from 1924-30, they organised several Commonwealth conferences, featuring an impressive range of delegates from around the world sympathetic to ideas of economic co-operation. By 1928 the Labour Party had accepted as party policy the bulk purchase by the state of food and other commodities from the Colonies and Dominions. This was a scheme pushed particularly by Johnston from 1924 onwards.

Johnston and the Commonwealth group faced opposition from many on the Left. Such opposition, where it was not based simply on anti-imperialist reflexes, was nourished by the favourable disposition of some Tories to Empire trading schemes. Baldwin, indeed, was quite taken by notions of bulk purchase and even complimented Johnston on his speeches on such topics in the Commons. To these Labour critics, too much attention to Empire – whatever the socialist rationale – was to play the Tories' game; Labour, in this view, would always come a poor second in any attempt to capitalise on issues of Empire, if only because the Tories could link such issues simplistically with patriotism. Moreover, there were those who thought that positive views of Empire ignored the continuing imperialist exploitation, especially of India and some African colonies.

To meet the cries of imperial exploitation, Johnston was to go on to develop his concept of Empire in relation to ways of increasing the purchasing power of those in under-developed colonies. By the end of 1924, however, his arguments had – in their earliest forms – stimulated fruitful debate, and given the Clydesiders another cause to rally round. For Johnston carried the support of the other Scottish Labour MPs on this issue.

Wheatley, in particular, was to take up such notions both in cabinet, and in his own newspaper, the *Glasgow Eastern Standard*, in early 1925. Wheatley and Johnston worked closely together on the question of sweated goods and Empire trading. In early 1925 they succeeded in getting the Labour Party to appoint a committee to consider the question of sweated imports. This committee's report, in Johnston's retrospective view, did more to shift the Labour Party away from 'Whiggery' than anything else.[9] In June 1925 the Clydeside MPs voted for Imperial Preference against the bulk of the Labour Party.

In response to this H. N. Brailsford, the editor of the London ILP newspaper the *New Leader*, expressed the commonest criticism of the Left when he accused Johnston and Wheatley of confusing the issue of sweated labour with ideas of Empire. In Brailsford's view, Labour had to construct a policy of preference regarding imports on the basis of labour conditions, not Imperial connections.[10] Such an approach avoided the controversies which notions of Empire provoked, but it also implied an unwillingness to co-operate with Labour governments in the Dominions, whatever the potential economic benefits from a socialist standpoint. To Johnston it seemed to be a case of spurning opportunities in deference to time-worn dogma.

Johnston's concept of an Imperialist federation of self-governing states bolstered his commitment to Scottish Home Rule. For Johnston and the other Clydesiders, life at Westminster only served to intensify their patriotic fervour. Commenting in *Forward* on the concept of a 'Scottish Renaissance' he wrote:

> . . . to any Scot who denies the existence of a Scots psychology I would prescribe a month's residence in London, and if he does not from the first week yearn for his fellow clay from ayont the Border: if he does not herd together with his kind, conscious that he is alien to the agreeable, forgiving, forgetful Cockney folk, then he is different from any travelling Scot I ever heard of.[11]

Agitation for Scottish Home Rule reached a peak in 1923-24. Much was expected in this direction from the Scottish Labour MPs. Huge demonstrations took place at which the rhetoric of speakers such as Maxton bordered on the inflammatory. Johnston, as we have seen, could be folksy, sentimental and dour in his Scottishness, but his was the most dispassionately reasoned advocacy of Home Rule at this time. As before, it sprang mainly from his concern with the social and economic decline of rural Scotland which had resulted in emigration on a significant scale. In Johnston's view the situation cried out for a Scottish parliament to undertake land reclamation, and to begin the process of repopulating the Scottish Highlands. He advanced his hardy annuals of afforestation and smallholding land cultivation schemes as a means to rural prosperity and self-sufficiency. Much of Johnston's strongest criticism of the Labour Government in 1924 concerned these questions; he lamented that their good intentions were not translated into positive action.

Like most people in the Labour movement, however, he was ambivalent about nationalism. He recognised how easily it could be perverted. Referring to an enthusiastic rally at Glasgow Green which Maxton had addressed, he wrote:

> Let us hope that the pageantry and the great demonstration last Saturday in Glasgow are indications not of a narrow, sterile, wha's-like-us pride, but of a resurgence of that national feeling which seeks to cherish the distinctive quality and genius which is ours by birth, by tradition, by social custom, and which if cherished and strengthened may be to the glory and profit of all mankind.[12]

In May 1924 George Buchanan introduced a Bill proposing Home Rule for Scotland within a federal Britain. Johnston seconded it. He proposed that Scotland should continue to be represented at Westminster in regard to Imperial affairs, until a general federal scheme was constructed for the Empire as a whole. Johnston thus argued that such Home Rule schemes were the only way to preserve the Empire. He accused the opponents of the Bill of seeking to use a central bureaucracy to destroy the distinctive national characteristics which were the life-blood of the Empire. In this way Johnston disavowed separatism while advancing the claims of a distinctive Scottish nationality.

Despite Johnston's eloquent appeal for the ultimate integrity of Empire, the Tory opposition talked the Bill out. The Scottish Labour MPs were furious, but MacDonald was relieved: he did not want the Government brought down on this issue. Johnston was not downcast by the setback. He considered the issue now to be a 'live one in politics'. He wrote:

> . . . The numbers of those who have in the past disposed of the issue by murmuring 'internationalism', as if absorption and strangulation were internationalism, and as if you ever could have the international without first the national, are rapidly fading away.[13]

III

The Government eventually fell in October 1924 in a climate of 'red scare' propaganda. Its proposal of a Treaty with Russia – guaranteeing a loan on the part of the British Government – united the Conservatives and Liberals in opposition. On top of this the Government decided to drop the prosecution of J. R. Campbell, a Communist journalist whose paper (the *Workers Weekly*) urged soldiers never to turn their guns on fellow workers. Asquith's motion calling for a Select Committee of Inquiry turned into a vote of confidence. The Government was duly defeated and another election held.

The election campaign then threw up another 'Bolshevist bogy': the Zinoviev letter, later to be proved a forgery. Johnston called it 'the most shameful electoral trick ever sought to be played upon the working class of this country'.[14] It may have been an effective trick for all that. Labour was reduced overall to 151 seats, the Conservatives storming back to power with 413. The Liberals trailed a weak third with forty. Johnston was one of Labour's casualties, losing in West Stirling to a new Conservative opponent by the slim margin of 299 votes. Johnston was not downhearted about Labour's Scottish performance over-all which – in terms of its share of the vote – was up to over forty per cent.

Shortly after the election E. D. Morel died. Morel, a pacifist who joined the ranks of the ILP from the Liberals after the war, had sat for Dundee. Johnston was nominated by the ILP to be their candidate in the subsequent by-election. Johnston was keen to have a break from parliamentary life, but he considered it a supreme honour to be asked to follow Morel. He had shared Morel's desire to improve the Labour Party's competence in relation to foreign affairs, and had greatly admired Morel's breadth of expert knowledge and international perspective. In this respect he had stood apart from fellow Clydesiders like Wheatley and Maxton whose attitude to Morel had been one of suspicion. They had resented the way that Morel – as an ex-Liberal – had criticised the Labour movement on foreign affairs.

Johnston, campaigning strongly on his Empire trading schemes and the issue of Prohibition, romped home in Dundee with a majority of 12,739 over his 'New' Liberal opponent, E. D. Simon. On prohibition Johnston called for a national referendum; he had clearly not lost hope of making the country 'dry' even if most other Labour temperance advocates had.

Johnston's main concern in the new Parliament was Labour's policy on Empire and international trade. He was eager for Labour to distinguish itself from the Liberals by taking a firm stand on the import of sweated goods. The test of sweated products, he stated, lay in the Washington Convention at which the Great Powers, including Britain, had agreed to recognise the principle of the forty-eight-hour week. Johnston argued that such a policy would raise the standard of living in the backward countries and help their unemployment problems. As MP for Dundee, Johnston complained that the city's jute industry could not compete with the jute produced by underpaid labourers in India. He was convinced that boycotting sweated goods would help to abolish sweating abroad. Moreover, Johnston believed that a rise in the purchasing power of workers in these countries would benefit British export industries and consequently diminish unemployment. It was these arguments that the Labour Party Committee on sweated goods, referred to above, endorsed in their final report in August 1925.

Such arguments were also developed from the under-consumptionist economic theory which had by now come to dominate the Labour movement in Britain. There were notable dissentients – such as Hugh Dalton – but, generally, such thinking was hardening into orthodoxy. Wheatley, of course, was a firm subscriber to this school, and he and Johnston continued to advance the most detailed and erudite propaganda from the Scottish end.

However, Wheatley had come to believe that the promotion of such a programme required either radical changes in the Labour Party, or the priming of the ILP to eventually take its place. The first option seemed unlikely. He, Maxton and most of the other Clydesiders had lost confidence in MacDonald. The latter's inept handling of the Zinoviev letter affair was, for them, the final straw. The sense of purpose with which they left St Enoch's in 1922 had been continually frustrated. Now they turned those frustrations on the Parliamentary Labour Party.

Johnston chose, in contrast, to identify more closely with the Labour leadership. After the defeat of the Government, he set about repairing relations with MacDonald which had been somewhat cool and strained for the duration of its time in office. In *Forward* Johnston defended MacDonald from his critics and con-

73

demned what he saw as 'personal vendettas'. He called for 'frank and open criticism' instead. By the latter part of 1925 MacDonald, at Johnston's promptings, was again writing regularly for *Forward* and using it as his 'pulpit'.

Johnston also eyed warily the intentions of Wheatley and Maxton in relation to the ILP. These intentions concerned the transformation of that party into a broad-based left-wing alliance which would embrace Communists. Fundamentally at odds with the Communist standpoint – particularly in relation to the Empire – Johnston was firmly opposed to this. So was Patrick Dollan, arguably the real power-broker in the ILP in the West of Scotland. As it turned out, Dollan was to thwart Wheatley and Maxton on this issue, and he remained a formidable opponent to their plans. Dollan and Johnston thus came to represent those in the ILP in Scotland who opposed any move which was likely to endanger the party's links with the Labour Party, or which called into question its support for it. For Johnston and Dollan, the ILP still had a vital propaganda role to play; moreover, it was still obliged to offer criticisms of the Labour leadership openly and honestly when it considered them due. To organise itself to be an alternative Labour Party, however, was something both men could not countenance. Wheatley and Maxton's plans were ambiguous in this respect, but it was clear nonetheless that something of this nature was afoot. A spirit of divisiveness thus crept into the Scottish Labour movement in 1925 over the old issue of the Labour Party's effectiveness. From the moment he had entered political life Johnston had argued the affirmative case; by 1925 it had become for him an article of faith. Wheatley had become restless to the point of losing that faith. The two men drifted apart just at a time when their thinking on major issues of the day had harmonised powerfully. Both were thinkers and both were doers. Ideas were flowing from both men and blending. Wheatley had passed a major piece of housing legislation in his time in government. Johnston had turned the Labour Party in the direction of his policies on sweated goods and Empire trading. The times seemed propitious for the kind of intellectual and propagandist direction both men were capable of providing. From 1925 onwards the prospect of such unity of purpose receded.

IV

Johnston's conception of Empire entailed self-government for its constituent nations and an end to exploitation. He rebuked J. H. Thomas for voting against a resolution at the TUC in 1925 which embraced these two objectives. Such actions, Johnston believed, only encouraged the Communists to step up their pro-paganda against the Empire as the cause of unemployment and poverty. To Johnston it was vital for Labour to repudiate this and to re-emphasise that capitalism was the cause – the Empire, on the other hand, could be a positive instrument to combat these ills. The Communists made much of Indian nationalism. Johnston countered by urging that India be granted Home Rule but encouraged to remain in the Empire.

Since becoming MP for Dundee, India had loomed large on Johnston's horizons. The economic competition in Jute led him to enquire into Labour conditions in India. 'Dundee capital', he wrote in *Forward*, 'migrates to India, erects factories there, and competes with the products of Dundee. In turn Calcutta is being ousted from the South American market by Czechoslovakia, and it simply is imperative that Dundee should know the actual facts about the competition that keeps its workers on the border line of starvation.'[15] Consequently, in October 1925, he travelled to India on a fact-finding mission, accompanied by John Syme of the Jute and Flax Workers' Union.

Johnston's three-month visit led him to investigate labour conditions, Indian trade union organisation, the Indian nationalist movement, and the effects of British administration.[16] He went with preconceptions: it is clear that his Empire-orientated schemes shaped the nature of his enquiry and his findings. Johnston did not go to India primarily to flesh out an indictment against Imperialism generally or British rule in India specifically. This is not to say that he was blind to injustices perpetrated by the British administration. For example, he railed fiercely against the Bengal Ordinances which resulted in detentions and deportations without trial of revolutionaries and nationalists. Such outbursts were not well received by the Viceroy, Lord Reading. Johnston was also shocked to find that the British administration permitted the display in cages of female prostitutes in a busy quarter of Bombay. He sought to scandalise the British public on the issue on his return, but failed to get the newspapers interested.

However, it is also the case that Johnston was in general impressed with the professionalism of the Indian civil service, and sympathetic to the problems involved in administering such a deeply complex and often mysterious society. He was decidedly unimpressed, on the other hand, with the Swarajists – the Indian nationalists. He was critical of their concentration on the issue of self-determination and what he saw as indifference to the wretched labour conditions of Indian workers. Such criticisms were welcomed by British officials.

Johnston went to India primarily to investigate labour problems and the prospects of schemes involving economic co-operation between Britain and India. He supported Indian Home Rule, but saw no prospect of its short-term realisation. As far as the urgent economic questions of the day were concerned, Johnston seemed to believe that, by attacking British rule, he would be obscuring their importance. For the moment British rule was a fact, and he viewed as priority the constructive use of it. He believed, as he was to argue later in his career in relation to Scotland, that Home Rule should follow economic improvements. He was unreceptive to the Indian nationalists' contrary argument that self-determination would be the basis for economic progress.

Johnston was dismayed by the working conditions and the poor wages of industrial workers and peasants, particularly in the textile and coal industries. That many of the Indian capitalists in these industries were Nationalists undoubtedly coloured Johnston's assessment of the Swarajists. Moreover, he was more astringently critical of these Indian masters than he was of their European counterparts. He clearly believed that most of the exploitation was carried on by natives; most European capitalists struck him as 'quite average decent fellows, bound to the wheel of a system they cannot themselves change'.[17] Johnston considered it much easier to get the latter to favour more humane labour conditions. The native exploiters he viewed as less amenable to humanitarian appeals. Thus, he looked to the development of the Indian Trade Union movement as the only effective remedy.

Johnston, however, could hardly have been surprised to find that trade unionism in India was generally in a rudimentary state. Not the least of the obstacles to its growth was the likelihood of government repression, but Johnston was more inclined to put the blame on the calibre of the trade union leadership. This, he reflected later, was largely of the 'lawyer-politician-careerist type'.[18] However, he did make exceptions in the cases of N. M. Joshi and R. K. Bakhale with whom he discussed the unionisation of textile workers in Bengal. In addition he sought to promote co-operative societies through the Co-Operative Organisation Association in Calcutta. Although union-building and the establishment of co-operatives were uphill tasks, Johnston was convinced that it was in these areas that a start had to be made. Only in these ways would the chronic labour conditions be improved. Moreover, such progress would help ensure that the Indian competition with British textiles and coal industries would be on 'fair, and not on slave, terms'.[19] This was the central purpose of Johnston's visit: to do something about the cheap labour which was threatening British standards of living.

Johnston returned from India at the end of January 1926. He immediately began the task of persuading British workers to contribute money – £100 was his target – to set up a textile union in Bengal. Johnston kept in touch with Joshi to this end, but if progress was made it was slow. Certainly, Johnston's hope of a textile union stimulating union growth in the coal industry did not come to fruition. Moreover, his efforts to strengthen the British Labour movement's links with India were largely made in vain.

Shortly after his return Johnston also published, along with Syme, a report of their tour. It was a damning indictment of the Indian jute industry and workers' conditions. However, it had another emphasis: that of the purchasing power of the Indian workers. As Johnston pointed out, their income per head was only £4 per annum and, as a consequence, they could not afford British goods. Thus British export trades suffered and unemployment at home increased.

Johnston thus linked the issues of unemployment at home and poverty abroad. He had gone to India with under-consumptionist notions about the lack of purchasing power both at home and abroad, and the remedies 'constructive Imperialism' could provide. His visit served to confirm him in this line of thinking and to give him ideas for the development of practical schemes. Much of Johnston's somewhat ethnocentric reaction to India was perhaps the result of his preoccupation with economic and commercial schemes which seemed to him to promise so much benefit to Britain as well as India. During the years 1926-28 Johnston promoted these schemes as vigorously as he had championed any cause in his career to date.

On 4 February 1926 Johnston replied to the King's speech

and addressed himself to the pressing issue of unemployment. He raised the issue of cheap labour in the colonies, and stressed the need to raise the purchasing power of the working class. Less predictably he suggested that unemployment should be considered as an issue above party politics. He advocated an all party conference or a House of Commons committee to investigate the problem and come up with solutions. The following month, also in the House, he further defined what he had in mind:

> I do not suggest at all a Select Committee for academic discussions, but to consider concrete proposals put up by local authorities, by some of our Town Councils and county councils, that are never voted upon in this House, and cannot be discussed in this House, because the congestion of business here makes it impossible that they should ever come before it.[20]

Johnston produced schemes which were designed to draw at least a measure of cross-party support. To Johnston the fact that a fifth of the human race were under British rule in India provided an outstanding opportunity. He suggested that the Government should gear its export industries to supply the Indians with modern technology in order to increase their purchasing power while providing work at home. He instanced the possibility of the engineering industry producing such tools as iron ploughs, automatic pumps and oil engines. Johnston suggested that the Government supply India, on the basis of tied loans, with such technology so that the increased agricultural productivity would raise the purchasing power of the Indians and increase the market for British goods. All this, he believed, would also stimulate the related heavy industries of iron, coal and shipbuilding. Johnston calculated that an increase in the purchasing power of India alone by $\frac{3}{4}d$ per head per week would yield an additional market for British goods to the extent of some £40 million.

Johnston packaged with these ideas the schemes he and the

Commonwealth Labour group had championed in relation to bulk purchase of Imperial imports. By selling these foodstuffs to the British people at cost price, the Government, according to Johnston's scheme, would be further increasing the purchasing power of the workers; markets at home and abroad would be boosted. To Johnston it all fell into placed beautifully; it even supplied the Labour Party with the most powerful of political promises – cheap food.

In August 1926 he took issue in *Forward* with Hugh Dalton's suggestions that the next Labour Government should make their priority the nationalisation of the mines, the Bank of England, the railways and electricity. Johnston's reply showed him at his most pragmatic and indicated the strength of his commitment to his Empire schemes. He argued that Labour's stay in power would be 'short and unhappy' if it took Dalton's advice. He reasoned that the benefits of the nationalisation schemes would not be apparent for some time and that the working class would thus be likely to become disillusioned. In such a context the capitalist press, financial corporations and other enemies of the party would be better able to weaken the party by their attacks. On the other hand, schemes such as bulk purchase offered the prospect of immediate dividends:

> If Mr Ramsey MacDonald would stick cheap food in the forefront of his programme he would sweep the country, and, what is more, when his chance comes again at the Treasury box he will be able to give the masses an early dividend and a dividend which will provide him with public support during the period in which his other and more difficult schemes of socialist reconstruction are maturing.[21]

This was Johnston's way of making the Empire appeal to the Labour Party. But he was also aware of the need to make socialistic schemes such as he was advocating appeal to other parties if unemployment was to be tackled immediately. To do this Johnston attempted to show that the end result would be a strengthening of the Empire. In a House of Commons debate on Empire trading he claimed that bulk purchase schemes would give working people a 'share in the Empire, a reason for desiring to build up the Empire and extend it'.[22] Johnston was attempting, at one and the same time, to give the Labour Party more practical credibility and to find a political consensus in relation to Imperial policies which would bring economic relief. In terms of practical detail, persistent propaganda and parliamentary preoccupation, Johnston was probably the leading proponent of this political course in the Labour Party in the late 1920s. There was always opposition from those who did not believe the Empire could be anything but exploitative, but bulk purchase schemes were nonetheless adopted as Party policy in 1928, and former Labour ministers like Tom Shaw began advocating Johnston's tied loan schemes in relation to India in the same year.

Johnston was not the brains behind the intricacies of bulk purchase; the thinking on these schemes had been done in the early 1920s by the economist E. F. Wise. But as Wise channelled his economic ideas into the ILPs programme to tackle unemployment and poverty – published as the *Living Wage* in 1926 – Johnston emphasised the potential of Wise's earlier plans. At the Commonwealth Labour conference in 1928 Johnston urged the delegates from the Dominions to turn their minds to bulk purchase schemes and to contrive ways of exchanging and marketing goods which would eliminate middlemen and speculators.[23] In relation to the latter issue, Johnston believed that the Empire Marketing Board could achieve much. He conceived of it as a means of co-operative marketing and of preventing market fluctuations, and of combating cheap labour. He envisioned the Empire Marketing Board as the sole importer of materials like jute, arranging with the Dominions to supply a guaranteed market and abolishing middlemen.

Johnston did not get his all party conference or select committee on unemployment. However, his arguments about the Empire did have a cross-party appeal. One Conservative duly impressed was Johnston's fellow Scot, John Buchan. In her biography of Buchan, Janet Adam Smith makes the point that the Scots Labour MPs had a different view of Empire from their English counterparts, that for them 'Empire-builders' meant those, often from Scotland, who literally were builders – of bridges, railways, roads and so on. They were thus less apt to see the Empire as the exploitation of subject races by public school educated Englishmen. 'The Empire', writes Smith in relation to the Scots MPs, 'was too big an affair to be left to the Carlton Club.'[24]

This was precisely Johnston's state of mind on the issue. In *Forward* in 1924 he had admonished his anti-Empire Labour colleagues in the following terms:

> We have to face the fact that every second household in this country has a brother or a son or a cousin in some British colony beyond the seas, and that these British Colonies are going Labour and Socialist, and only on the assumption that we are politically and economically daft can we be expected to regard our kindred beyond the seas as no more to us than Bornean Headhunters or Esquimeaux.[25]

This spoke for the Scottish Labour MPs, including Wheatley and even the demogogic Maxton. In September 1927 Johnston accused Baldwin of giving the impression that the Empire was bound up with the fortunes of landlordism and capitalism; he was determined that the Tories should not appropriate the Empire as a political issue and thus undercut his attempts to portray it as an instrument of progress. While he welcomed support from individual Tories for his Empire schemes, Johnston considered that the party was still too likely to foster notions of an Empire of exploitation.

Johnston had some success in turning the Labour Party more purposefully towards Imperial economic answers to the problems of unemployment and poverty. On an informal level he found common ground with members of other parties. His notion of taking unemployment out of the party arena was somewhat ahead of its time. His schemes built imaginatively and constructively on the economic thinking of the time. But tangible results were limited. 'Constructive Imperialism' appealed to many, but there was a paralysis creeping across the political arena in relation to Britain's economic problems. Bold remedies invariably brought a cautious response. Britain's return to the gold standard in 1925 pointed up the strength of financial orthodoxy. The Labour movement, moreover, was traumatised at a time when Johnston needed it to be clear-headed.

V

The General Strike of May 1926 found most eminent political figures in the Labour movement in the role of anxious onlookers. Johnston was no exception. He had anticipated a major industrial struggle on the part of the miners from the time of the Government's climb-down over the question of a subsidy to the coal industry in August 1925. The miners and the Trades Union General Congress (TUGC) seemed to have won a notable victory in the struggle over reductions in wages and the number of working hours. The subsidy was for nine months and the Government used the time to prepare for all-out confrontation. Johnston, at the time of 'Red Friday' when the Government gave in, considered it a phyrric victory. He feared that those who favoured industrial to political struggle would once again gain credence for their tactics. Johnston did not look forward to confrontation in a context in which the Labour movement still lacked political power. He urged Arthur Cook, the miners' extraordinary leader, to ensure against defeat by starvation and to organise food supplies in colliery districts. 'Are plans being prepared', inquired Johnston earnestly, 'for setting fishermen at work barrelling salt herrings?'[26] Johnston, indeed, half-believed that most predicaments in life were hopeful on a meal of salt herrings!

Political Labour leaders were divided in their assessments of the strike which ended after nine days with nothing achieved for the miners. Most, like Wheatley, blamed the TUGC for surrendering tamely. Others, like Maxton, took heart from the extent of working-class solidarity displayed. For Johnston it bore out all his sense of foreboding and only served to confirm him in his opposition to those who gave primacy to industrial methods of struggle. However, he was disappointeed at the TUGC's lack of courage once the strike had started, and *Forward* moved passionately behind the miners who chose to stay out after the strike had been called off. *Forward* had in fact been prevented from appearing during the strike.

The ILP did not play a significant role in the General Strike, but it had been busy nonetheless. Early in 1926 the interim report of the Party's commission on the Living Wage – comprising E. F. Wise, H. N. Brailsford, Arthur Creech Jones and J. A. Hobson – was published with the title 'Socialism in our Time'. This report, and the final *Living Wage* blueprint published later in the year, embodied under-consumptionist economic thinking by setting forth proposals to raise the purchasing power of the working class. Such proposals included family allowances, the reorganisation of depressed industries and compulsory wage rises, state control and regulation of credit, state control of incomes and prices, and the adoption of centrally planned investment spending. The latter proposals reflected the influence of the economist J. M. Keynes. The *Living Wage* was in fact something of a fusion of Hobsonian and Keynesian economics. The need for control of the supply and prices of imports was also stressed. All in all it was a plan designed to increase living standards under capitalism to facilitate the transition to socialism.

Socialism in Our Time and the *Living Wage* were both documents that Johnston might have been expected to back strongly, given his own efforts to argue the case for much of what they contained. Certainly *Forward* offered lavish praise, but this reflected the enthusiasm of Hughes (responsible for most editorial duties at this time) rather than Johnston. Hughes indeed wrote a stinging rebuke to MacDonald after the latter had peremptorily dismissed *Socialism in Our Time*. MacDonald by now was totally at odds with the ILP which he considered a dangerous nuisance. His opposition to the proposals – and the indifference of most of the trade unions – meant that they made little impression on Labour Party policy-making.

This frustrated those around Wheatley and Maxton who saw the ILP as more than the propagandist vehicle MacDonald wanted it to be. In the aftermath of the General Strike Wheatley and Maxton considered decisive action more urgent than ever; they perceived MacDonald and the Labour Party as being absorbed into Baldwin's political consensus in which financial and economic orthodoxy precluded any chance of socialist policies making an impact.

Johnston, by contrast, continued to defend MacDonald. This made for a rather uneasy editorial partnership at *Forward* between Johnston and Hughes, with the latter also unhappy about the quality of MacDonald's weekly column. But MacDonald considered *Forward* important and was suitably grateful for Johnston's generous words. In January 1927, for example, he wrote to Johnston thanking him for a front-page article in his defence, and going on to write: 'It is not at all a question of myself, but the movement. I care not whether Smith, Brown or Jones is nominally the head of it. If his authority and personality are constantly being belittled the mischief is not that he begins to assume the appearance of a guy, but that the whole movement does the same.'[27] MacDonald returned Johnston's compliments at *Forward's* twenty-first birthday celebrations. One of the reasons for the paper's success, he said, had been that 'Tom Johnston had discovered and perfected a new form of journalism, the snappy paragraph. Johnston had the amazing ability of picking out a paragraph from a speech or an article and by adding two or three lines of shrewd comment, sarcasm, or deep philosophical reasoning turning it to the service of the Movement.'[28]

Johnston still believed in MacDonald's leadership qualities and his popular appeal. He considered MacDonald too valuable an asset to lose. He believed that the combination of MacDonald's leadership and a powerful but simple message was Labour's best chance. As has been noted, Johnston considered that the schemes in relation to the Empire which he tirelessly advocated had the virtue of being easily reduced to core concerns such as cheaper food. Moreover, they provided a means for Labour to play – in a constructive manner – the traditionally Conservative patriotic card. Johnston thought that the political ground was narrowing. He did not fear Labour absorption or 'co-option' by right-wing or centrist politics, but he did see the situation as a test of Labour's credibility. The trouble, in Johnston's view, with the ILP programme was that its intellectual quality outran its propaganda uses. For all Johnston's encouragement of ideas and hard thinking within the Labour movement, he was always, at the end of the day, concerned with what made good propaganda, won votes and strengthened Labour politically. He never allowed himself, in the excitement of policy planning or the pursuit of ideas, to lose sight of realistic objectives. Johnston's mind was as fecund as most of the Labour movement's thinkers in this period, and he desired more of the Labour party in relation to the schemes which he championed than what he got. However, Johnston, unlike Wheatley and Maxton and many others on the

Left, did not allow himself to become frustrated to the point of courting political impotence. Johnston reacted soberly to the sobering experience of the General Strike. Desperation seemed to overcome Wheatley and Maxton.

There was no split between the latter men and Johnston. Johnston, indeed, had paid a handsome tribute to Maxton on his becoming ILP Chairman back in 1925, and his respect for Wheatley was undiminished. In essentials both men were still thinking along the same lines. Johnston still seemed confident that the ILP would again ride in harness with the Labour Party. In response to Philip Snowden's advice in January 1928 to the ILP to disband, Johnston put the case for the ILP while obliquely criticising its lurch from realities:

> Both the administrator and the visionary are necessary to the complete political instrument . . . if the vision perishes the party will die; and on the other hand, if the Party loses touch with the realities of the hour and becomes a mere collection of Holy Men living in a dreamland, it will be of as much use in the world as are the Straiter and Stricter Brethren who can pay little attention to the drains for thinking of the golden pavements.[29]

To Johnston's dismay, the Cook–Maxton manifesto of 1928 in which Wheatley too was involved intensified divisions within the Labour movement. The manifesto was ostensibly a reaction to the Mond–Turner talks betweeen trade unions and employers, an indication, in the view of Cook and Maxton, that there was a dangerous political drift to the centre. Johnston was at first satisfied about Maxton's motives, but both he and Hughes regretted the 'confusion' which the manifesto had created. Later he criticised Maxton's reluctance to carry on his campaign under the auspices of the ILP. This, he argued, only resulted in speculation about splits.

The manifesto campaign in any case came to nothing. Patrick

Dollan again expertly marshalled opposition in the Scottish ILP, and his and Johnston's pro-Labour Party line still held sway. As the Cook–Maxton agitation was at its peak, the Labour Party published its new programme: *Labour and the Nation*. This document took no electoral chances, and was roundly excoriated by the Left. Johnston agreed that it was 'a sort of dog's breakfast in which there are scraps for every palate', but he supported it on balance. He simply did not see at that moment a working-class electorate which hungered for a more distinctively socialist programme.

VI

The late 1920s also saw Johnston produce pamphlet literature in support of the mainstream Labour electoral drive. *The Year 1926 Under the Tories* and *Life Under the Tories in 1927* were aimed at 'shaking the Tory working man into sense' with the kind of ferocious debunking employed in earlier pamphlets such as the *Huns at Home*. By August 1927 *Forward* claimed that over 100,000 of the former pamphlet had been sold after only six months. Early in 1929 Johnston published *The Success of Nationalisation* with a foreword by Arthur Henderson. Much of this pamphlet was inspired by Johnston's trip, in late 1928, to Canada where he was greatly impressed by such experiments in nationalisation and co-operation as the hydro-electric scheme at Niagara and the Canadian Wheat Pool. Such propaganda epitomised Johnston's concern for simple, clear and hard-hitting arguments which did not sail over the heads of people who, as he was fond of saying, did not have a Latin dictionary at their elbow.

Johnston was also prepared to defend *Labour and the Nation* in debate against no less an adversary than J. M. Keynes. Keynes, in 1928, provided the economic thinking behind the Liberal *Yellow Book* proposals with which Lloyd George sought a return from the political wilderness. This debate – while vigorously enough contested – served mainly to show that there was much common ground between the participants. Johnston admitted that many of the *Yellow Book* proposals could be voted for by socialists 'with both hands'.[30] The *Yellow Book* was an impressive intellectual document; whether it was effective electoral propaganda only time would tell.

Johnston's central role in support of Labour's campaign and the *Labour and the Nation* programme confirmed him in an identification with the British State. Johnston was now looking to the State as a means of economic planning and restructuring, as indeed was Wheatley. Both had helped to lead the Scottish Labour movement in what was, in effect, a British approach to economic problems, Home Rule rhetoric notwithstanding. Johnston continued to campaign for a Labour government using British state power to bring about socialist change.

Scottish Home Rule, therefore, became something of an awkward issue in relation to Johnston's overall outlook after 1926. It was consistent with his ultimate ideal of a federated Empire, but it sat uncomfortably with the other economic schemes which Johnston wanted action on sooner. He also recognised the increasing integration of Scottish trade unions into the wider British movement, and the indifference, if not hostility, of the many English or English-based colleagues he had come to know and work with through his parliamentary career.

In 1927 the Reverend James Barr (a Scottish Labour MP) proposed a new Scottish Home Rule Bill which provided for Dominion Status and the withdrawal of Scottish MPs from Westminster. Johnston seconded it, but he was later to admit to having had serious reservations about the Bill, particularly in relation to the withdrawal of MPs. This provision aroused opposition from Labour members in the House, and the Bill met the same fate as Buchanan's in 1924: it was talked out. Reaction in the Scottish Labour movement varied this time from mild irritation to outright relief. Enthusiasm on the issue had ebbed distinctly.

The Bill's failure resulted in the formation of a Nationalist Party in Scotland, and in denunciation of the Scottish Labour MPs as ineffectual by Roland Muirhead, who was still a *Forward* director. Johnston was sensitive to these attacks, for his commitment to Scottish affairs had been total since his entry to Parliament. However, the reality of his being bound up with a British political and economic strategy in a British context left him compromised. He could only attempt to influence Scottish legislation in the manner of his exhaustive assault on the Tories' Scottish Local Government Bill in 1928; or make a symbolic gesture such as voting – along with several other Scottish Labour MPs – against the New Church of England Prayer Book. On this latter issue – which was no business of Scottish Presbyterians – these votes actually proved decisive. Johnston, however, was pulling away from the idea of Home Rule being a prerequisite for radical economic change in Scotland. His perspective in India was certainly not consistent with it. Moreover, Johnston had no sympathy with the separatist aims of the Scottish Nationalists; his Empire enthusiasms reflected a willing acceptance of the overriding concept of 'Britishness'.

In the general election of June 1929 Labour was returned to office for the second time as a minority government. This time, however, they were the largest party. Johnston was returned for his old seat of West Stirling with a comfortable majority of 4,590. Labour's electoral tactics had paid off with the best result in their history. Johnston, as one of the most effective propagandists, might have considered his 'reward' of the Under-Secretaryship for Scotland rather meagre. He accepted nonetheless. Contemporaries in the Party believed he should have been in the Cabinet.[31]

Johnston's grasp of the realities of British political culture left him well placed in 1929 to play a role in shaping the future.

Wheatley was now on the outside looking in, embittered. Maxton was well on his way to becoming Westminster's token rebel, loved not feared. None of the Clydeside contingent of 1922 attained as prominent a political position as Johnston, although Shinwell was to come to office in 1930. The political culture was distinguished by a strong anti-theoretical bias and a distrust of heavyweight programmes such as the *Living Wage* and the *Yellow Book*; notwithstanding his interest in, and engagement with, the challenging ideas of the time, Johnston was eminently suited to it.

4 Financiers and the nation (1929-1935)

Johnston took office with no illusions about the extent of the new government's mandate. It did not cover the enactment of socialist policies; to achieve that was, in his view, the task of *Forward* and other Labour publications. In the meantime Johnston saw the Government's brief as reducing unemployment, and producing results in the areas of peace, pensions and housing. He took office willingly, in view of his new responsibilities to Scotland. However, a relative lack of ambition to climb the 'greasy pole' was still a feature of his outlook. On signing off temporarily as editor of *Forward* – Hughes took charge – Johnston declared: ' . . . however immersed one may be for a time on other duties, I cannot forget that the *Forward* is my bairn. If the need were to arise I should drop the other duties without hesitation and return, uncontrolled and untramelled, to its service'.[1] He still considered himself, first and foremost, a journalist and propagandist.

In contrast to the pragmatic acceptance on the part of Johnston and a majority of Scottish ILP MPs of the limitations imposed on a minority government, another faction, led by Wheatley and Maxton, favoured the pursuit of all-out socialist policies. They were prepared, of course, to see the Government thus brought down, so that a clear majority for socialism could be sought at another election. Macdonald made it clear from the start that there was no prospect of such a course being adopted. Consequently, Maxton, Wheatley, Kirkwood and others prepared to carry on a critical campaign against the Government from the back benches. They were, in fact, opposed to any ILP members taking office. In view of such an uncompromising stance it was unsurprising that their criticism should be targeted, before long, on Johnston.

Wheatley by this time had acquired his own mouthpiece in the local newspaper, the *Glasgow Eastern Standard*, and it was this paper which became the main vehicle for attacks on Johnston's performance as Scottish Under-Secretary. In October 1929 it harassed Johnston over the issue of wages paid to relief workers on an outdoor scheme at Lennox Castle in Stirlingshire. The *Standard* alleged that Johnston turned down a scheme which would have paid workers 55s a week in favour of one that paid 40s. Johnston angrily condemned the story as a 'damned lie', and the paper produced no evidence to support its allegation. In November, the *Standard* contrived a personal attack on Johnston over the provision of free coal for the poor, and accused him of having no knowledge of the under nourished children of the Gorbals in Glasgow.

At the turn of the year Wheatley himself put the blame squarely on Johnston for the worsening unemployment situation in Scotland. He focused on two matters: a plan to build a mid-Scotland ship canal, and a proposal to take over a Lesmahagow works to provide employment for miners in the treatment of coal. Wheatley asserted that Johnston had declared the former 'cut and dried' but had not delivered his promise; and he insinuated that Johnston was dragging his heels in respect of the latter. In addition to this, Wheatley asked when Johnston was going to take action in regard to the range of schemes he had advocated in opposition, schemes such as those designed to increase the purchasing power of Empire peoples, experiments in co-operative marketing, and the development of afforestation. In April 1930 Wheatley picked holes in a Slum Clearance Act for Scotland for which Johnston had been largely responsible.

From someone like Wheatley who well knew the political and administrative difficulties involved in the process of government, such a campaign was surprisingly petty and small- minded. It was probably motivated in the first instance by Wheatley's by now rabid hostility to Macdonald's philosophy of gradualism. In this context Johnston was simply the most obvious Scottish target. Yet the personal nature of the attacks was unmistakable, an indication perhaps that Wheatley had felt betrayed by Johnston and his refusal to join a Wheatley-inspired ILP front to change the nature of Labour politics in Britain.

Certainly, there was little of substance in Wheatley's charges. The mid-Scotland ship canal scheme could not go ahead without a geo-physical enquiry, and the Lesmahagow works proposal had never been anything more than a remote possibility. Furthermore, Johnston had only been a matter of months in office before schemes were already well advanced in co-operative marketing and afforestation. After months of ignoring the sniping from the *Glasgow Eastern Standard, Forward* slammed Wheatley and his 'vendetta' in January 1930. With Hughes in control, *Forward* was less pro-Macdonald, but it was far more critical of the ILP rebels.

The split in the ILP ranks over the new Government was nowhere more apparent than in Scotland. *Forward*'s pages were filled with acrimonious exchanges between Patrick Dollan, an ally of Johnston's, and John Paton, secretary of the ILP and very much in tune with Wheatley and Maxton. At the Scottish ILP conference in January 1930 the rebels found themselves in a minority, and Hughes imperiously announced that 'purely romantic sentimental socialism is at a discount'.[2] Johnston used the occasion to play down controversy over the question of ILP members voting against the Government – as Maxton and company did in relation to the Unemployment Insurance Bill – and to stress instead the over-arching issue of the ILP's relationship to the Labour Party. He called on the ILP, for as long as it remained an integral part of the Labour Party, to abide by the latter's tactical decisions. This was consistent with the drift of Johnston's political approach through the 1920s, but it still represented a contrast to the period of the first Labour Government when Johnston himself had caused trouble for Macdonald and had indeed voted against the Government.

The issue of ILP members voting against the Labour Government could not be wished away, despite Johnston's inclinations. It intensified the rifts between the parties, and brought disaffiliation closer. At the national ILP conference at Birmingham at Easter 1930 the NAC insisted that the Party's MPs accept and act on the policies of the conference. In turn the Parliamentary Labour Party resolved that no member could vote against the Government. All but eighteen of the ILP's 140 MPs followed the PLP line. In doing so, Johnston stated his position clearly in a letter to Paton:

> . . . I cannot see how a member of the Government can be expected to vote against the Government of which he is a member, either at the bidding of a group in the Party, or of the NAC. I can undertand the ILP declining to affiliate to the Labour Party, and declining to allow its members to accept office in the Labour Party, but I cannot understand the ILP affiliating, and at the same time binding its representatives to vote if called upon against the considered decisions of the body to which it has affiliated. The position appears to me to be untenable and indefensible . . .[3]

Johnson thus ceased to be a member of the ILP group in parliament.

By the time he did so the ILP had suffered a mortal blow. On 12 May 1930 Wheatley died, having suffered poor health for some time. It is indeed likely that recurrent illness exacerbated his sense of political disillusionment and left him uncharacteristically bitter in his final years. The ILP and the Left, in Scotland and in Britain as a whole, lost its most formidable advocate. Johnston paid tribute, the recent squabbles forgotten and the promise of their joint talents unfulfilled.

II

It is a misnomer to say that Johnston was the junior minister at the Scottish Office from 1929-31. Although he was officially subordinate to the Secretary of State, the craggy Fifer William Adamson, Johnston in practice ran the show. Adamson recognised the younger man's talents, energies and ideas, and gave Johnston the scope to express them. Johnston also took on parliamentary responsibilites to a greater degree than any Scottish under-secretary before or since. He answered questions in the House more frequently than Adamson, and generally took a more positive role in piloting through legislation. Officials and civil servants looked primarily to Johnston for direction. Adamson, of course, had the ultimate responsibility, and he gave Johnston unfailing backing.[4]

For Johnston the priorities in relation to Scotland were housing, unempoyment and agriculture. He considered that the Government's minority position made it unwise to attempt to dismantle the recent Local Government Bill which he had strenuously opposed. Similarly, Johnston took the view that it could not be the occasion to introduce a Home Rule Bill. Such legislative minefields would have taken up all his time and precluded action on the urgent social and economic questions.

With its economic dependence on the export industries of shipbuilding and engineering, Scotland was particularly vulnerable to the international crisis which set in after the Wall Street crash of October 1929. In the first six months of Labour taking office, unemployment in Scotland increased by some 200,000. It

continued to rise alarmingly in 1930, especially in the industrialised West of Scotland where almost twenty five per cent of
the registered work force were idle. Outside of Northern Ireland,
this was the most severely depressed part of the United Kingdom.
The consequent lack of purchasing power discouraged the establishment of new domestic consumer industries, most of which
emerged in the south of England.

Johnston was not short on ideas to combat the unemployment
problem. He was in fact put on the Unemployment Committee
set up by Macdonald and headed by J. H. Thomas, the Lord
Privy Seal, after the Government took office. The work of this
committee will be discussed below. However, both as a member
of this committee and as Under-Secretary for Scotland, Johnston
was to be largely frustrated in his attempts to bring his schemes
to fruition. Treasury policy was sceptical of the job creation
schemes advanced in a climate of growing financial uncertainty,
and the Chancellor, Philip Snowden, was rigid in his adherence
to this orthodoxy.

Johnston's central concept in relation to job-creation was a
Scottish Development Board. He saw the establishment of such
a Board as a necessary mechanism for stimulating, attracting and
co-ordinating new industrial investment. He envisaged it as
operating along the bi-partisan lines of the Empire Marketing
Board, which he was by now involved with in the area of marketing. Johnston also saw the Development Board as a means of
giving new direction to the Scottish tourist industry. In July 1929
he submitted a memorandum to Macdonald proposing the
development of Scotland as 'a health centre and a tourist resort',
and appealing patriotically to Macdonald to recommend his
scheme to Snowden. Johnston advocated that the Development
Board be given £50,000 per year to stimulate tourism: he argued
that jobs would be created in response to increased tourist traffic.
In addition, he proposed the building of a scenic road round

Its all in hits. A road here, a Board there. –

Loch Lomond, another project which would immediately yield substantial employment.[5] Johnston got Macdonald's sympathy but had to do his own pleading with the Treasury. In the event he failed to get his way despite the relatively modest sums he was requesting. It was an instance of MacDonald's reluctance to confront and overrule Snowden, a recurrent feature of this Labour Government which fuelled its problems. Johnston suffered from the financial orthodoxy of Snowden and the pusillanimity of Macdonald. It should be noted that a Scottish National Development Council was set up in May 1930; however, it proved to be largely a cosmetic body.

He also suffered from the creeping desperation of the country's mood. Without hard cash for work schemes, Johnston had to look for ways in which Scotland could tap its economic potential. Again, his store of ideas was rich, but few of them offered short-term methods of cutting unemployment. Such ideas largely drew on Johnston's long-held conception of a rurally-repopulated Scotland, agriculturally co-operative and self-sufficient. His one concrete suggestion in relation to the depressed Glasgow region was that Scottish imports should be shipped directly to the Clyde rather than through London, thus creating jobs and lowering prices. However, this required the co-operation of merchant importers and bankers, which Johnston never found time to secure. As his tenure of office wore on Johnston's optimism about Scotland's *long-term* future did not console those for whom job creation schemes were being continually 'considered' but not delivered.

More tangible results were achieved in other areas. Much was done for the fishing industry, especially in improving harbours. A land drainage act was passed, which brought improved farming conditions. Johnston inaugurated a co-operative egg marketing scheme on the island of Skye, and an experiment to supply free milk to schoolchildren in Lanarkshire, both of which provided models for further similar schemes. A bill was passed to meet the grievances of smallholders and tenants, and a start was made in sequestering land hitherto used as deer forests. An important rural housing act was also passed in 1931 before Johnston was moved from the Scottish Office.

It was, however, the Housing (Scotland) Act passed in 1930 which was the most notable achievement of the ministry in the time of the Labour Government. This was popularly known as the Slum Clearance Bill. More than any other previous measure, including Wheatley's Housing Act of 1924, this Bill provided for a long overdue assault on Scotland's infamous urban slums. The Bill gave local authorities the grants and the powers to undertake slum clearance operations and to rehouse families. A family allowance principle was incorporated: the bigger the family to be rehoused the bigger the grant. Although the Government was anxious that the local authorities should implement the provisions of the Bill, a clause was nonethless inserted which gave the government power to compel negligent local authorities, on health grounds, to build houses. Much of Johnston's time in fact was spent in conference with local authorities thoughout Scotland, explaining the Act and urging them to avail themselves of it. Johnston claimed that no local authority, however harassed financially, could be excused for not tackling the problem of slums. Moreover, he saw it as a companion piece of legislation to the Wheatley Act, and to the Rural Housing Act which followed.

Johnston played a major role in drawing up the Bill and his parliamentary skill was shown at its most dextrous in seeing it through the committee stages. As a significant piece of legislation it was subjected to a searching scrutiny at every stage, and amendments proliferated on the vexatious issues of rents, local authorities, compulsory purchase orders and legal problems. It was, in many ways, a more complex piece of housing legislation than the Wheatley Bill. For Johnston it represented an opportunity for large-scale municipal socialism in relation to housing. His commitment to local government had never wavered, and he was determined to devolve as much power to them as he could without jeopardising the ultimate aims of slum clearance and house-building. He reserved compulsory powers to the government, hoping never to have to use them. If local authorities made use of the Act it was Johnston's belief that a form of Home Rule would be in operation. In this regard he was never less than sensitive to Home Rule appeals, and probably felt somewhat sheepish about having to go back on past pledges to Scottish self-government.

It was only after some time that the efficacy of the Act could be assessed. In all important respects it proved a success. By 1938 some 50,000 families had been removed from insanitary housing to more modern habitations. In general the local authorities in the areas of greatest need took advantage of the Act without much pressure. In addition, successive administrations up until the war continued to operate the Act, a testimony to the excellence of its planning and the breadth of its scope.

Johnston's period in the Scottish Office ended in March 1931 when he was asked to take over as Lord Privy Seal. All in all Adamson's decision to give Johnston the leeway he sought was vindicated. In the context of a Depression and an unco-operative Treasury, his record was impressive. At the time, however, it was unavoidable that he should have been judged – and judged less favourably – on the most pressing issue of the day: unemployment.

III

The 'Thomas Committee' on unemployment comprised two other ministers as well as Thomas and Johnston, namely George Lansbury, the First Commissioner of Works, and Oswald Mosley,

Chancellor of the Duchy of Lancaster. Lansbury was a close ally of Johnston's inside the Labour Party, the two having worked together in the Commonwealth Labour group. Mosley was young and charismatic, bursting with ideas and very much in a hurry to put them into action. He believed that the economic crisis was his opportunity.

However, the Committee's role and purpose were from the beginning uncertain. Thomas was in charge, but it was unclear whether the other three were simply there to give advice when requested or to co-ordinate more positively a coherent policy. Johnston and Lansbury certainly attended to their own offices first and were not able to spare the time that such a topic as unemployment demanded. Indeed Johnston, as late as October 1929, was unaware whether he was a proper member of the committee or 'part of an interested audience'. He told Lansbury that he only attended meetings on the request of Adamson.[6] To compound the sense of confusion and lack of co-ordination, Macdonald had also set up an interdepartmental committee of civil servants on the problem of unemployment. Thomas presided over this committee but his three advisory ministers were not, initially, invited to attend.

It appears, in the course of the first few months of the Government, that the original committee effectively ceased to function in any meaningful way. In his memoirs, Johnston claims that it only met twice in six months.[7] The focus of discussion instead shifted to the interdepartmental committee which Lansbury and Mosley started to attend from 27 June, and Johnston from 8 July. By this time key decisions had been taken and a bureaucratic consensus against large-scale public works schemes in effect established. Thomas in this respect was in the pockets of the civil servants, particularly Sir Horace Wilson.

It was just such a programme of public works, particularly on roads, that exercised the energies of Mosley, the most involved of the three with the unemployment problem. Promoting schemes which had been part of Lloyd George and the Liberals' *Yellow Book* appeal, Mosley ran up against the obstacles of local authorities on the one hand, and Thomas and the bureaucrats on the other. With the backing of Johnston – expressed in a joint memorandum in October – he urged that the Government treat unemployment as a national and not a local problem and take responsibility for the immediate implementation of national road schemes.[8] Opposition came from other departments, must notably the Ministry of Transport, headed by Herbert Morrison. Many ministers disliked the idea of overriding the local authorities. Above all Treasury policy considered such schemes financially unsound. Mosley and Johnston were thus rebuffed, and relations between Thomas and his advisory ministers deterioriated.

It was not the only rebuff the latter suffered before the year was out. The Government had also promised to combat unemployment by means of a retirement pensions scheme. Thomas, in June, appointed a sub-committee on the matter consisting of Johnston, Mosley, Lansbury and selected civil servants. By September the three ministers had come up with a scheme to pay £1 a week to a single man and 30s a married man for all sixty-year-olds provided they retired within six months. Johnston claimed it would take 280,000 off the dole at a stroke. The plan was submitted to the Cabinet in November without Thomas's backing. It too was rejected.[9]

A frustrated Mosley responded to such setbacks with even bolder action. In January 1930 he produced a detailed memorandum setting out both short and long-term solutions to the unemployment problem, and calling for a revolution in the machinery of government to achieve them. The memorandum was prepared by Mosley on his own, but he intimated to MacDonald that it had the general agreement of Lansbury and

Johnston. Certainly it was the case that, in the wranglings which followed, both men backed Mosley and did not conceal their dissatisfaction with Thomas. Mosley had kept Lansbury and Johnston aware of his intentions, but had been vague in his dealing with Thomas. To add to the latter's injured pride, Mosley showed the memorandum to the economist Keynes for his comments before submission, and probably arranged for it to be leaked. Thomas felt he had been publicly humiliated, and Mac-Donald considered his complaints of more moment than the memorandum itself.

A Cabinet Committee duly rejected the memorandum in March 1930. Mosley, along with Lansbury and Johnston, were given a single meeting to argue their case. In opposition to it, Snowden emphasised the Treasury axiom that economic recovery could only come through the revival of Britain's export trades. This school of thought feared that spending on short-term expedients could be money squandered at the expense of the export trades' long-term health. Mosley contended that he too was looking to the future; he argued that British industries had to undergo rationalisation to make them competitive, but that the resulting rise in unemployment had to be met by a public works programme of some kind to maintain purchasing power and consumer demand in the home markets.

Mosley was not the kind of politican to suffer a major setback quietly. He resigned on 20 May during a ministerial conference at which Johnston spoke highly of his (Mosley's) talents and entreated his colleagues to make use of them. However, at the same meeting, Johnston made it clear that he was opposed to Mosley's revolution in government and the diminishing of the power of local authorities which it would entail. Mosley's resignation, in fact, was taken without consulting either Johnston or Lansbury, and both were unimpressed by it. Johnston stated afterwards to Hugh Dalton that he felt Mosley had stormed out just when they were beginning to win on 'essentials'.[10] After Mosley had left the meeting Johnston also suggested that the Government 'rope in' Conservatives and Liberals into the administration. He envisaged Lloyd George in a 'Council of State for agriculture', and likened such arrangements to the non-party status of the Public Accounts Committee. MacDonald, however, stated that at such a crisis point the other parties would not come in.[11] In his letter to MacDonald in support of the Mosley Memorandum on 24 January, Johnston had also canvassed this idea of an all-party committee to examine relief projects.[12] Overtures to the Liberals and the Conservatives had in fact been made by the Government by the time of Mosley's resignation, and negotiations were to continue on and off. However, the snags were plentiful and mutual distrust and suspicion rife.

Against the background of a dramatic rise in unemployment and mounting anxiety in the country, Mosley delivered a stirring resignation speech in the House on 28 May. In it he gave eloquent expression to the proposals in his memorandum, but also expanded significantly on some of these proposals. Thus he argued more trenchantly against the policy of encouraging what he called 'a swollen export trade', and advocated instead a policy of developing home markets and protecting them with import controls. He also reasserted his readiness to appropriate powers and responsibilities from the local authorities. The speech was a theatrical *tour de force* and was rapturously received.

Later on in the same debate Johnston addressed himself to the issues in Mosley's speech.[13] He proclaimed himself in agreement with much of Mosley's programme, which meant in effect the short-term proposals regarding a national roads scheme, retirement pensions, and the raising of the school leaving age. However, Johnston also felt that Mosley, in parts of his speech, 'did himself less than justice'. Johnston begged to differ on two major issues: the development of the export trades and the position of the local authorities.

Johnston regretted Mosley's deprecation of the export trades. He argued that it was most definitely in the country's interests that they should flourish, and he cited the example of fishing as an industry which would provide more employment if it was properly developed. Johnston's plan for fishing concerned the promotion of the herring trade with Russia. Mosley's attitude to other export trades, such as in bicycles, brought this rejoinder from Johnston: 'It is precisely the development of our export trade in such matters as cycles which has been one of the most hopeful features of recent years in our Empire trade development; and Coventry and other towns are today living upon the very fact that the West African native has been taught to ride a bicycle.' In saying this Johnston was, rather incongruously, making precisely the same point that had been made by Snowden against the Mosley Memorandum, which Johnston in general supported.

In relation to the local authorities, Johnston had always displayed a reluctance to tamper with their powers. However, in this speech, his attitude became one of unequivocal antipathy to the idea, and is again hard to square with his earlier support for Mosley, except in terms of his anger at Mosley's resignation. He said:

> I can conceive of no greater turmoil than would be created in this country than by the ruthless attempt at overriding the powers, the duties and the privileges of the local administrative bodies in this country. However anxious we may be, for example, to deal with the problem of slum housing and the problem of building new houses, it is an extremely difficult matter indeed for a Central Executive, particularly a Central Executive elected from one side of partisan politics in this country, to override the wishes of the elected representatives on the local authorities, who are composed for the major part of other political parties, and the mere threat

that a Labour government would seek to override the measures taken by the County Councils composed entirely of members of political parties represented by the Opposition in this House, would have results which can surely be better imagined than described.

Here then was the real problem as Johnston saw it: partisan politics. Despite going along with Mosley's short-term plans for tackling employment, he had apparently taken a view quite different from the latter as to the main obstacles to that objective. While Mosley saw the problem as one of defective machinery of government, Johnston despaired of the fetters inherent in a continuing system of party rivalry at national and local level. Johnston believed that many Conservative local authorities were being unco-operative regarding the Labour Government's schemes. He said so to Macdonald in the aftermath of Mosley's resignation.[14] However, such a view did not lead him to share Mosley's remedy; Johnston was not opposed to the powers of the local authorities as such, simply to the partisan politics which prevented them making the best use of such powers to combat unemployment.

In his speech of 28 May Johnston went on to develop this theme. He spoke of the 'obstructions and delays inherent in a partisan political struggle', and gave instances from his own experience as Under-Secretary for Scotland of local councils making difficulties. He finished with a powerful peroration against such politics:

> Until we can get unemployment and its emergencies regarded as an all party question in this House; treated as questions were treated in the emergency of the war; obstruction swept away; the pettifogging delays which take place in this House over ordinary legislative proposals abolished; an all party committee responsible to parliament, making recommendations to parliament – unless the House can rise to such a conception of its duties, I do not believe it is possible quickly to expand the area and the scope of relief works in this country.

Johnston had favoured unemployment being taken out of the party political arena as early as 1926. However, he had by now developed this inclination into something of a practical creed. Moreover, he wanted other matters, particularly agriculture, also considered on an all-party basis. As Under- Secretary for Scotland he instituted a weekly conference of MPs from all parties to discuss Scottish issues, a process he was to take significantly further in his later career as Scottish Secretary. Johnston got on well with Lloyd George, and used *Forward* to keep pushing the notion of a Labour–Liberal alliance at this time. His relations with the Scottish Conservative MPs were also cordial and co-operative. Three Scottish Tories of this period, Walter Elliot, John Buchan and Robert Boothby, were outstandingly able and talented, and Johnston seems to have felt personally more at home with them than with erstwhile colleagues in the ILP. Perhaps more importantly, Johnston relished his work in 1930 as Chairman of the marketing committee of the Empire Marketing Board. This all-party body promoted agricultural marketing schemes close to Johnston's heart, and seemed to show that substantial practical measures could be taken the more quickly for the relative absence of party considerations.

Johnston's arguments were plausible and the factors which influenced him potent, but there seems nonethless to be an element of glibness and naïvety in his recommendations of bi-partisan practices. He seems not to have considered that such problems as unemployment might have been the result of political as well as economic decisions. The decision to return to the gold standard in 1925 was at least in part political, and while it might have pleased the city, it weakened the export industries and caused unemployment. It is curious, therefore, that Johnston, who was shortly to go on the offensive against High Finance and who prized so highly the contribution of the export industries, should have been so sanguine about unemployment being able to command a political consensus. In many ways it was the political or the 'class' issue *par excellence*. There was little prospect of it ever being depoliticised in a parliamentary democracy such as Britain, as coming events were to indicate.

On one level Johnston could still be found delivering a socialist critique of the capitalist system. In his speech of 28 May he decried it thus: 'Production today is unregulated. It is unregulated by the necessities of consumers; it is chaotic and it is a scramble of gluts and shortages here and abroad.' Johnston was fond of contrasting his socialist conception of trade – that Britain could only be prosperous if its trading partners were prosperous and able to buy her goods – with what he saw as the self-destructive practices of undercutting and underselling and of dumping surpluses on other countries' markets. This, of course, echoed his arguments on empire trading which he had advanced since the early 1920s. On another level, however, Johnston seemed to take the view that until international socialism gained sway and such concepts had been generally accepted, solutions in constituent nations had to be found on a pragmatic basis. It made little sense to Johnston, in the light of financial crisis and declining markets internationally, to blame unemployment on any government or political party. Nor did tariffs appear to him to offer any remedy; there were higher rates of unemployment in protectionist countries such as the USA and Germany. In this sense too he parted company with Mosley.

It thus appears that Johnston's earlier support for Mosley had been based solely on their shared belief in short-term measures such as retirement pensions and public works, and on a respect for Mosley's undoubted ability. Perhaps in the cause of putting up a united front along with Mosley and Lansbury, Johnston had suppressed his doubts and objections. However, he could have felt under no obligation to conceal these on 28 May, given Mosley's peremptory resignation and the widespread rumours that he was going to break with Labour.

Neither did Johnston accept Mosley's analysis of the situation as an either/or question. In Mosley's view Britain had to rationalise its industries, build up its home markets and protect them, and provide schemes for the unemployed; it was either that or dependence on the export trades, on world markets and thus on international finance. In keeping with his personal dynamism, Mosley tended to pose issues in such a cut-throat way: it was always either positive action of the kind he suggested, or certain drift to disaster. This reflected a razor-sharp mind and a decisive disposition, but it also over-simplified complex issues and conjured up some specious polarisations.

Johnston believed that, on an all-party basis to secure local authorities' co-operation, national work schemes should be provided, and measures such as retirement pensions introduced. However, in the face of an international crisis, this would at best only reduce unemployment. For those who were still unemployed, maintenance was the only answer. Johnston did not think that Britain should retreat from her role in world trade or that she could insulate herself in the way Mosley seemed to be suggesting. He shared, in essentials, the conventional view that Britain's export industries had to be revitalised. His continuing advocacy of 'constructive imperialism' strengthened him in this view. Moreover, he was very conscious of how vital the export industries were to the economic life of Scotland, and of trade union strength in this sector of the economy. But Johnston did not, as a corollary to this, disparage home consumer industries. His advocacy of public works schemes and better standards of maintenance were based on what he saw as the need to maintain domestic purchasing power. Nor was he anything but favourable to economic diversification. In addition, Johnston was firmly in favour of state intervention and the State's assumption of the responsibility for economic welfare. This of course was simply traditional Labour policy, but it contrasted with the Treasury's continuing bias in favour of *laissez-faire* which Snowden did not challenge. For Johnston, at this juncture, it was 'work and maintenance' and support for both domestic and export industry.

Johnston thus seemed to want to have it all ways. Was his approach less realistic than Mosley's, or that of Snowden and the Treasury which rejected a loan-financed national public works scheme? In retrospect it might be strongly argued that the nature of Britain's economy could not respond to an even-handed approach which attempted to foster all-round growth. In hard economic terms, measures to stimulate the export side ran the risk of harming the domestic side, and vice versa.[15] However, this notion of the incompatibility inherent in the 'dual economy' was by no means self-evident at the time; nor is there clear evidence that either of the competing schools of economic thought referred to were correct in their respective diagnoses and prescriptions. Johnston was not being woolly-minded or opportunist; he had strong reasons for urging advance on all economic fronts. Given the complexity and the apparent intractability of the international economic situation, perhaps his positive, yet non-dogmatic and open-minded, approach was not inappropriate.

In the wake of Mosley's resignation MacDonald attempted to supply a more coherent and purposeful government approach to unemployment. Ironically, some of the changes might have been to Mosley's liking. Thomas was moved to the Dominions Office and Vernon Hartshorn took over as Lord Privy Seal. A panel of ministers presided over by MacDonald himself was set up to deal with unemployment. This panel was served by a Secretariat and was linked to the recently established Economic Advisory Council (EAC). The latter was another device for bringing together ideas and formulating policy, and the EAC comprised some of the most seminal economists of the day, such as Keynes. Mosley watched the Government continue to struggle, launched his 'Manifesto' (based on the memorandum), and then left the Labour Party in February 1931. He formed the 'New Party' which did not take long to metamorphose into the British Union of Fascists.

On 14 March 1931 Johnston was elevated to the Cabinet and the office of Lord Privy Seal after the death of Hartshorn. It was an important appointment; like Thomas and Hartshorn before him, Johnston was now responsible for tackling the unemployment problem. He thus took his place on the panel of ministers concerned with the question. Almost immediately Johnston discovered how little scope he would have to manoeuvre: the Treasury objected to the financial commitments involved in an unemployment scheme in connection with the Fourth and Tay railway bridges in Scotland. On a more positive note he also took charge of the issue of extending Export Credit Guarantees to British firms which traded with Russia. After much haggling Johnston was able to persuade the Unemployed Grants Committee to insure the firms concerned for a further two years, an achievement which brought valuable orders and maintained jobs in several export industries. High on this success, Johnston in May 1931 publicly announced that Russian orders for iron and steel were about to be finalised, a premature move which brought down the wrath of Macdonald upon his head.[16] Nevertheless, Johnston's success in this regard was widely noted by his peers.[17]

On 16 April 1931 a Conservative censure motion against the Government was debated in the House. It fell to Johnston to make the main defence of the Goverment's record and its policies.[18] He claimed that public works schemes were in operation employing, directly and indirectly, 226,500 men. He pointed to the Government's legislation on matters such as slum clearance and land drainage and reclamation. He made much of his own work on Export Credits. However, Johnston was forced to talk for long spells about schemes under consideration, and he was plainly more at ease in addressing questions of long-term recovery. In this latter respect he was both orthodox and unorthodox, on the one hand looking to an improvement in world trade to stimulate the export industries, on the other stressing more off-beat visions of his own regarding tourism and the conversion of coal into oil. It was a speech, however, which was clearly sceptical that the Government could do much more than hope for an improvement in the international situation. Like the rest of Labour Cabinet, Johnston's overriding commitment to parliamentary gradualism permitted little in the way of an adventurous approach. Johnston had by now retreated from his more radical stances of 1929-30 in support of Mosley.

The Tories were scornful of his speech. Replying, Captain Crookshanks recalled that Johnston had dubbed the *Labour and the Nation* programme a 'dog's breakfast', and he applied the same description to Johnston's speech. Lloyd George was much kinder. He praised Johnston warmly and expressed the view that he had 'a very firm grip of the position'. Lloyd George took thirty Liberals into the Government lobby for the vote, and the motion was duly defeated. This was in fact a manifestation of a tacit alliance between the Government and the bulk of the Liberals which had been carried on since the end of 1930. It also fuelled speculation that Lloyd George and other leading Liberals would enter the Government, an eventuality which would have pleased Johnston. Certainly he was in close touch with Lloyd George and the Liberals: in June 1931, for example, the Cabinet minutes record that he was instructed to confer with Liberal representatives on the subject of the government's proposed Unempoyment Insurance Bill.[19] However, Liberal sympathy notwithstanding, the world was closing in on the Government.

IV

The international financial crisis in summer 1931 put the squeeze on the Labour Government. Snowden determined to balance the budget, and a committee under Sir George May was set up to consider ways of cutting government expenditure. The report of this committee recommended cuts of 97 million, 67 million of which was to come from cuts in unemployment benefit. Panic reigned as the Bank of England claimed that its gold reserves were dwindling. The Government's fidelity to orthodox economic canons precluded the option of going off the gold standard. Crisis enveloped the Cabinet as it debated ways of making the cuts. Johnston, for his part, recommended the highest rate of reduction, namely twenty per cent, of the salaries of ministers and other public servants.[20] MacDonald and Snowden pressed for cabinet acceptance of cuts in unemployment insurance quite independently of the bankers.[21]

In the event the Cabinet split over the proposal to cut unemployment benefit by ten per cent. Johnston and eight others voted against; eleven were in favour. Johnston, Lansbury and Greenwood had been against from start to finish. The Government fell and MacDonald resigned, only to bow to the appeals of the King to form and lead a national government with the opposition parties. Snowden and Thomas followed him into this administration. Arthur Henderson, the Foreign Secretary, led the dissentients, and Johnston afterwards praised his stand. Notions of a 'Great Betrayal' by MacDonald came after his expulsion from the Labour Party on 28 September; in the immediate aftermath there was sympathy for him in the Labour ranks.

Johnston, through the pages of *Forward* and elsewhere, immediately turned on the 'international moneylenders'. It was they, he claimed disingenuously,[22] who insisted on the cut in unemployment benefit despite the Labour Government's willingness to balance the budget in other ways:

> They made it perfectly clear that it was not a balanced budget they
> wanted, but a budget balanced by methods which they specified
> . . . they insisted upon a ten per cent cut at the unemployed as a
> condition of their lending credits to save the pound sterling from
> collapse. They intimated that unless the unemployment benefit
> insurance rates were reduced by ten per cent they would be prepared
> to see a financial smash in Great Britain.

Johnston went on to attack the May Committee report for not
highlighting the massive slice of the budget taken up with interest
on the National Debt, one of Johnston's oldest propagandist
themes. He argued that an appeal could have been made to the
holders of war debt to reconvert at lower rates of interest. Why,
asked Johnston, should Britain's heaviest item of expenditure be
sacrosanct? Large blocks of the war loan, he claimed, were exemp-
ted from tax burdens. He concluded by saying that the Government had been 'dictated' to by American financiers.[23]

Johnston employed these arguments in a rhetorical vein during
the debate on the National Economy Bill on 11 September. The
City of London financiers, he alleged, had wasted the nation's
resources and had then come to the Government to ask it to
restore confidence on its (the city's) terms. In addition he con-
fessed that:

> For the first time, I think, in my life, I have doubts in my mind as
> to our ability to evolve . . . as to our national ability to evolve
> gradually and with progressively less suffering into a social order
> wherein the appalling poverty, tragedies and miseries of our time
> can be no more; but I am certain of this, that the steps now being
> taken in this House will not make it easier . . . You are creating a
> class war spirit.[24]

The sudden force of the crisis, for a long time kept at bay,
had stunned Johnston temporarily out of notions of consensus

politics, and thrown him back to a class perspective. Conservatives and Liberals assumed, once more, the characteristics of the ruthless defenders of ruling-class interests. Johnston the crusading socialist propagandist replaced Johnston the pragmatic politician. However, the resurgence of Johnston's radicalism should not prevent notice being taken of his increasing tendency towards Treasury orthodoxy when in office. This took place from around the time of Mosley's resignation, and was pronounced enough to convince MacDonald in March 1931 that Johnston was a 'safe' choice for the crucial post of Lord Privy Seal. Johnston accepted the view that the budget had to be balanced and the gold standard maintained; it was simply that he could not swallow unemployment cuts. He was, moreover, not opposed to the idea of a National Government, and would probably have welcomed one which sought to balance the budget in another way.

Johnston reacted quicker than most in the shell-shocked ranks of the Labour Party, and his counter-claims to the national media attacks on it provided a powerful rallying cry. Johnston was now truly a national figure, and his contentions, as an ex-cabinet minister, were given attention far beyond the Labour Party. Inside the Labour Party his standing was reflected in the vote, taken on 7 September, for the executive of the Parliamentary party. Johnston was elected with the highest vote (151) ahead of Lansbury and Dalton. At the Labour conference in October, Johnston denounced the 'camarilla' of international financiers and pledged that a future Labour Government would restore the cuts and wipe away Poor Law tests. A general election now loomed in the same month. For Johnston it represented a chance for Labour to stand for the establishment of national control over finance; to this end he was shortly to urge a Labour Finance Committee to examine the obstacles to the nationalisation of the banks.

His and *Forward*'s election campaign was typically vigorous,

Thomas Johnston

but in a fearful climate the task was hopeless. Labour in Scotland was decimated, as it was throughout Britain. Johnston himself was a casualty, losing in West Stirling by 1,819 votes. This defeat put paid to his chances of becoming leader of the Labour Party, a prize which fell to Lansbury. If Johnston had been returned it is doubtful whether he would have stood for the leadership, but, if he had, it can with hindsight be argued that he would never have had a stronger claim.

Out of Labour's paltry total of fifty-two seats in the new Parliament, only seven were Scottish (four of them ILP). The National Government took office with an overwhelming majority. Tariff reform, which Johnston still generally opposed, quickly followed; but so also did the conversion of war loan, and, in the longer term, planning and Keynesian economic policies. In September the Government had gone off the gold standard, an option which the Labour Government had been led to believe was too risky.[25] Economic catastrophe did not result, but the Depression nonetheless continued.

V

Johnston's New Year message to *Forward* readers at the start of 1932 was an old Jacobite saying – 'whatever men dare they can do'. It sounded somewhat ironic coming from a member of the late Labour Government who, in the end, had dared to do very little more than his colleagues. However, seated behind his editorial desk, Johnston was always prone to a romantic flush. Freed from the constraints of government the celtic warrior spirit was allowed more leeway. And there were indications, such as speech on the National Economy Bill, that his faith in gradual socialist evolution had been shaken.

If, however, the test of the latter was disillusionment with the Labour Party and a more favourable disposition towards the 'pure socialism' of the ILP, Johnston was no candidate for conversion. Certainly he waxed bold about what a reorganised Labour Party should aim for – the cancellation of reparations, the conversion of war loan, an inheritance tax, the drastic reduction of tariff barriers, a national investment board to control credit, international disarmament – but he also condemned attacks on the existing political, industrial and economic machinery, namely the Labour Party and the trade unions. Johnston put it straight to the ILP that 'co-ordination and direction of the Socialist propaganda inside the Labour Party, and not the creation of a rival and duplicate working-class machine' should be 'the duty and the opportunity of the ILP'.[26] At the Scottish ILP conference in January the question of disaffiliation – although decided in the negative – dominated proceedings. Johnston was the butt of some satirical comment from delegates, and he complained that such attitudes made 'unity impossible and comradeship difficult indeed'.[27]

In March 1932 Johnston stood as Labour candidate at a by-election in Dunbartonshire. When first approached, he was extremely reluctant to do so. Having taken over again as editor of *Forward*, Johnston considered that he had an important job on his hands to restore Labour morale and produce propaganda to meet the crisis. Moreover, *Forward* was by now struggling economically, having made trading losses and having suffered a drop in circulation. Johnston clearly had major surgery to perform on his 'bairn'. On top of this he was getting increasingly involved in the running of the City of Glasgow Friendly Society (he became General Manager later in 1932), a body in which he propagated some novel ideas about life assurance. Nor was he only preoccupied with polemical jounalism; he was also engaged in writing a history of his home town of Kirkintilloch, which had made him its first freeman in July 1931.

Eventually, however, he was persuaded to stand, and he managed to cut a Tory majority of 12,000 to just over 5,000. Indeed his chances of victory would have been very high had Nationalist and Communist candidates not opposed him. He fought the campaign on a wide range of issues, foreign and domestic. The League of Nations was held up as the embodiment of the 'internationalism and pacifism' he claimed to stand for; the burden of the War Debt was stressed and his remedies proffered; Scottish Home Rule was supported with the proviso that it would not of itself cure economic ills; the Export Credits Insurance Guarantee Scheme was recommended as a measure to tackle unemployment, liberal reference being made to his own working of the scheme in relation to Russia and the benefits this had brought to Scottish firms; and the abolition of the Means Test for unemployment benefit was unequivocally urged, Johnston hotly denying that the Labour Government had anything to do with its introduction. In response also to an accusation by MacDonald that Johnston was being disingenuous over the issue of Free Trade, Johnston declared that he had never been 'an absolute free importer' – he had opposed free importation of sweated goods – but continued to reject tariffs as an economic remedy. Johnston's references to Macdonald in the campaign were more in sorrow than in anger. Moreover, *Forward*, somewhat curiously, ran advertisements for MacDonald's National Labour Committee publication, *Newsletter*. Clearly, *Forward*'s financial situation must have been grave.

From the time of the Labour Government's fall, Johnston made *Forward* a forum for debate on economic and financial questions, above all others. He was determined, like the Labour movement generally, to make up for previous vagueness on finance and blind acceptance of the bankers' stipulations. In true *Forward* tradition he invited all comers to the debate. No monetary scheme or financial reform was too outlandish to be considered. He himself floated ideas which resulted in controversy. One such was a proposal that the state buy a portion (he suggested 1,000 million) of the War Loan with new notes and destroy it. When readers wrote to protest that this would lead to rampant inflation, Johnston posed the question of whether the destruction of one form of paper debt (the interest bearing war bonds) and its substitution by another (non-interest bearing Treasury notes) necessarily meant inflation, and, if it did, what steps could be taken to obviate inflation. In raising such questions Johnston was taking great delight in being economically heretical, and challenging orthodox canons of finance; he was encouraging his readers to question the bankers and the moneylenders and to scrutinise their immutable axioms. In this latter respect he probably succeeded, even if his own arguments bore the mark of what one reader called a 'confidence trick'. Certainly a wide range of people participated in such controversies, from learned economists and Labour MPs, to 'lay' readers.[28] Johnston touted in particular the economist Professor Frederick Soddy whose work had inspired his War Loan proposal and who, in Johnston's view, was one of the few authorities on economics who grasped the importance of the National Debt in the country's financial economy.

In July 1932 Johnston welcomed the new Labour Party finance banking programme, saying that it proposed the nationalisation of the Bank of England; the establishment of a National Investment Board; and emergency powers to deal with any attempt at sabotage or the creation of panic by the 'private financial institutions'. He argued that such control of banking and finance would give a Labour Government the scope for planned development of national resources on socialist lines. Such a programme, Johnston claimed, was precisely what *Forward* had supplied 'shot and shell' for in propaganda efforts.

The Labour Party may thus have been making some genuinely radical and socialist noises, but the ILP remained unimpressed. At a special ILP conference in Bradford at the end of July the vote went in favour of disaffiliation from the Labour Party, a decision which dismayed, but hardly surprised, Johnston. Gloom-ily, he predicted that the ILP would embark on a 'fratricidal' war with the Labour Party, and he was not wrong. However, the most pressing worry for Johnston, Dollan and indeed the majority of the Scottish ILP who had opposed disaffiliation, was that the ILP was still the predominant Labour political organisa-tion in Scotland. The Labour Party would now have to build up its strength from the very flimsy organisational base it possessed. To this end the energetic new Secretary of the Scottish Labour Party, Arthur Woodburn, directed his efforts. Woodburn saw eye-to-eye with Johnston on most issues, and shared absolutely his views on organisational structure and propaganda activities. At an affiliation conference in the wake of the ILP conference, Johnston advised his listeners to confine their future activities to propaganda and to avoid duplicating the Labour Party's elec-toral work. Out of this conference came the Scottish Socialist Party (SSP), formed to carry on what they thought was the true ILP propaganda role. Johnston joined but he was nowhere as enthusiastic as Dollan and others; in common with Woodburn he feared that it might become a rival organisation which would hinder rather than complement Labour Party operations in Scotland. In the event the SSP did not long maintain its initial momentum.

The Left in Scotland was in fragmented confusion. Just at this juncture the Communist party made a strong and partly successful bid for the leadership of the unemployed, and the hunger marches and demonstrations which they organised left the Labour Party looking somewhat aloof and indifferent. To Johnston it was the politics of desperation filling an organisational vacuum. His antipathy to the Communist Party grew in proportion to the inroads it made into working-class support. But the unemploy-ment problem could permit of no aloofness; it averaged twenty-five per cent in the depressed west of Scotland, significantly above the UK average of just over sixteen per cent. For once, Johnston might be said to have transgressed his own dictums about propaganda being judged by its usefulness, its clarity and its positive guidance. As the dole queues lengthened, *Forward*'s financial expatiations got ever more intricate and convoluted, and may often have spread more confusion than enlightenment.

However, *Forward* also had a duty, as Johnston saw it, of addressing the complexities of the country's economic problems, and *Forward*'s saturation coverage only reflected the extent to which such questions were the primary concern of the Labour movement in Britain in this period. Painstakingly, if tortuously, Johnston developed his arguments for converting the national debt from an interest to a non-interest-bearing basis, and for increasing consumer demand. He was at his best, however, when he attempted to simplify solemnly:

> The problem before our generation is to translate the full implications of democracy into our economic life, so that not only shall men be politically upon the same plane, but that each shall have an equal and indefeasible title to his share in the social product.
>
> Somehow or other there must be arranged a steady increase in the buying power of the people. For the day of scarcity is over: the day of abundance has come.
>
> And the finance mechanism that will not permit the abundance to reach the tables of mankind is one that already stands condemned.[29]

VI

In April 1933 Johnston officially handed over the editorship of *Forward* to Emrys Hughes, although he continued to contribute weekly articles. He was preparing a book which he hoped would summarise usefully the financial issues he had raised in *Forward*, and which would contribute to the formulation of a Labour Party programme on finance.

Johnston envisaged such a programme as providing for the increase in the consumption of goods. He wanted money driven out of immobilisation in the public debt into active use in the markets. Johnston had been increasingly drawn by the debates over financial questions into a preoccupation with consumption, surpluses and the home market. Increased productivity and wealth, he suggested, should be distributed in a National Dividend, and, to be at its maximum, that dividend meant socialism.

But Johnston was greatly influenced by non-socialist forms of national dividend, especially the Social Credit schemes of Major C. H. Douglas. Douglas, a Scotsman, advocated the organisation of credit on behalf of society by the Government, and the prevention of credit control by international financiers. Johnston, not suprisingly, saw attractions in this, and considered that the scheme held out the inviting prospect of the buying power of the nation being increased with every annual increase in production. Johnston seemed also to be satisfied that Douglas's scheme would not involve inflation, and that the end result would be increased employment through increased purchasing power and not increased productivity resulting in glutted markets and unemployment. He was nonetheless well aware of the criticisms Douglas attracted from the left: that the schemes did nothing to plan or reorganise industry, or to socialise ownership of the land and industrial capital. Douglas himself was a declared anti-socialist, but Johnston argued that those on the Left should still study his ideas and examine seriously the National Dividend as a method of distributing surplus produce.

In the summer of 1934 Johnston published the book, *Financiers and the Nation*, which was the product of his study and research since the fall of the Labour Government. Sidney Webb wrote the preface, saying that the book was 'of great public service' and praising Johnston's exposure of financial skulduggery, and his assessment of 'remedial measures'. The book was a rather uneasy mixture of Johnston's usual journalistic polemic and more scholarly and didactic exposition, but its overall impact was powerful. Financial swindles of the past were brought to the reader's notice in a style reminiscent of *Our Noble Families*, and much of this part of the book had already appeared in a more rudimentary form in either *Forward* or *Reynold's News* for which Johnston wrote a weekly column in 1931-32. The weightier side of the book saw Johnston analyse and appraise impressively various remedial schemes such as Douglas's Social Credit, and ideas then current across the spectrum of British political and economic opinion. On the idea of a National Investment Board, for example, Johnston argued the case for it as an instrument to control and plan the nation's capital resources; however, he also offered measured criticism of the conception of it held by Liberal economists such as Keynes:

> To begin with, they omitted to place in the forefront, the safeguarding and protection of the small investor from the shark, through a visaing of the new capital issues; they omitted to safeguard the municipalities (the biggest public borrowers); they unnecessarily interfered with the work of the National Debt commissioners; and their proposal to issue National Investment Bonds for all sorts of enterprises not state owned, would speedily land any Government which sought to operate the proposal in a vast crop of credit trouble.[30]

A National Investment Board, basically conforming to the Keynesian model, was to be central to the Labour Party policy document of 1934, *For Socialism and Peace*.

Johnston also included in the book an account of the 1931 crisis, sticking rigidly to the line that the Government had been killed by high finance and got the blame for the financiers' mess. At one stage in his account Johnston stated that a majority of those who opposed a cut in unemployment benefit were prepared to accept a revenue tariff upon the import of manufactured goods. It is not made clear whether he was one, but there may have been some substance to MacDonald's charge during the Dunbartonshire by-election. Certainly, in Johnston's critique of the National Government's solution to the crisis he seems implicitly to accept the principle of tariffs:

> Instead of saving the gold standard and balancing the budget, by means of a voluntary conversion of the public debt to a lower rate of interest (as they had to do later when the gold standard had gone in any case), and by cancelling the derating subventions given to wealthy and prosperous firms, and by a revenue Tariff and by similar measures, the new Coalition government borrowed abroad the £80,000,000 at $4\frac{1}{4}$per cent, plus heavy commissions, and it forced considerable and drastic economies upon the poor. Standards of living everywhere were reduced.[31]

In conclusion Johnston urged his readers to reject the notion that high financiers knew best; they had, he contended, been wrong about reparations from Germany and their effects, about the Gold Standard in the 1920s, and about the claim in 1931 that re-suspension of that standard would being economic ruin. In terms of its brief – to explain economic and financial ideas and theories, and to shatter the aura of greater wisdom around financiers – *Financiers and the Nation* was a rapier-like propaganda weapon, not without some sophisticated touches.

Implicit in much of Johnston's outlook on financial questions was an endorsement of the concept of central planning. This was, for example, a feature of the vigorous support he gave in 1933 to Herbert Morrison over the latter's public corporation scheme for London transport, which opened the door to central planning as well as preserving the independence of private business. However, Morrison's scheme had many critics in the Labour movement, and this was a debate which pointed up the extent to which ideas about planning were still at best half-formed. Moreover, they were not ideas on which Labour had a monopoly: planning, in the first half of the 1930s, exerted a strong appeal across the political spectrum. Indeed the National Government put Morrison's London Passenger Transport bill on the Statute Book. Johnston was aware of the growth of 'middle opinion' groups and of a climate of opinion favourable to more efficient centrally-planned direction of industry and the guidance of 'experts' and technocrats. Indeed he was a signatory to the manifesto in May 1934 of the 'Liberty and Democratic Leadership group', a precursor of the pro-planning 'Next Five Years Group' which came into existence in February 1935. Both were groups of no definite party bias. Despite this, however, Johnston was not, relatively speaking, very expansive on the subject. He seemed to take a general sense of the concept in his mental stride, considering planning ideas to be merely commonsensical rather than profoundly radical. Even a trip to the USSR in 1934, about which he wrote at length in his memoirs, did not provoke him into an enthusiastic exploration of questions and theories of the kind he had launched into finance. Johnston was more interested in the plight of religion in Russia and in the easy availability of marriage and divorce; as a pioneer of planning, Russia was not the inspiration to him that it was for other Labour politicans and thinkers. Johnston – in relation to planning – was a passive supporter and little more. In 1935 he paid much attention to Lloyd George's 'New Deal' package of measures – Lloyd George after all had been enthusiastic about *Financiers and the Nation* – but Johnston did not concern himself with a discussion of their implications regarding planning; he dwelt instead on the by now familiar topics of consumer credit and market surpluses.[32]

Johnston, by the mid-1930s, was absorbed in the economics of the home market. He believed now that socialists had to put the emphasis on the distribution of products rather than the right to work. His most cherished vision had become that of marketing boards turning surpluses into organised channels of distribution to the needy in society. At a conference of the SSP in March 1935 he moved a resolution to amend the marketing boards by giving them statutory powers to dispose of surpluses of goods for distribution as an experiment in national dividend. This aroused a lively debate in which several critics warned of 'the Fascist danger from Douglasism'. Johnston was not daunted by the links between social credit schemes and Fascism; he saw such schemes as providing a way of feeding the hungry and pointing to 'the road of extended distribution to the socialist commonwealth'.[33] Johnston had of course tried for years to popularise schemes to market surpluses in the context of empire trading, but now his stress was on schemes directed at such bodies as the Milk, Potato and Meat Boards at home. He urged that credits be created to enable distribution at reduced prices of the surpluses of these marketing boards, instead of having the surpluses destroyed, and rejoiced that proposals to this end were endorsed by a Labour Party Committee of Enquiry, which included the economics experts Evan Durbin and Hugh Gaitskell, in its report to the Labour conference in October 1935. This preoccupation with the home market also led him to call more stridently for new domestic industries to be set up in depressed areas. This form of attack on unemployment had now largely replaced his former sterling defence of the export industries. It was a significant change of emphasis, although he still held out the hope that there would be a revival in international trade. However, to Johnston's dismay, it was to be a revival in international hostilities which boosted the old industries.

VII

Johnston, in the belief that the next election would be fought
on the issue of finance, spared no effort in examining the complex
questions involved on the subject. In the years 1931-35 he
epitomised the way in which the Labour Party as a whole did
some hard thinking in the wake of the traumas of 1931. Johnston
was not afraid to draw attention to ideas which were unpopular
in some leftish circles – ideas like the Douglas Social Credit
schemes – or to dissent from fashionable ideas such as the
nationalisation of the Joint Stock Banks. He probably pushed
social credit schemes harder than any other major figure in the
Labour movement. This was because he was seduced by the
notion that such schemes might offer a quick and effective answer
to chronic poverty. In this he was undoubtedly mistaken, but it
is easy to see how social credit could appear to be a means to
such an essentially socialist end. Moreover, in the context of the
depressed early thirties when suggested remedies for unemployment only sounded convincing if they were long-term remedies,
it perhaps made electoral sense to explore more urgently possible
means of wiping out hunger and raising living standards in the
meantime.

However, Johnston's actual influence on the Labour Party –
on its thinking and its policy-making – was probably less significant in this period than his experience and standing in the Party,
and his energetic propaganda activities, merited. To a large extent
this was because Johnston returned to Scotland after the defeat
of 1931 and virtually stayed put there. His by-election defeat in
1932 probably came as something of a relief to him at a time
when he saw himself playing several vital roles – not all of them
political – in a Scottish context. Nor had he ever made any secret
of his detestation of travelling up and down to London and having
to stay there for days on end. The result of this was that Johnston

was effectively cut off from colleagues such as Hugh Dalton or Hugh Gaitskell who, like him, were very much 'coming men' and who used this period to advance their careers in the Labour movement significantly. In 1932, Dalton wrote regretfully in his diary that Johnston was 'marooned' in Scotland.[34] In fact, Dalton, most unusually, wrote consistently in a kindly and admiring vein of Johnston. He found Johnston amusing in the way he recounted cabinet gossip, the source of which was usually Adamson, in the 1929-31 period.[35] This indicates a mischievousness and humorousness about Johnston which by no means everyone who came into contact with him appreciated.

Another factor rendering Johnston's influence less marked was that *Forward*, while still an influential paper, had suffered a drop in circulation by 1931, and was to undergo even harsher times in the wake of the ILP disaffiliation from the Labour Party. Moves were afoot in 1932 for the *Daily Herald* to take over *Forward*, but they fell through. Traditionally the paper of the Scottish ILP, *Forward* never really recovered from the split in this party which began to open up in the mid-1920s. The ILP breakaway, as noted earlier, was more damaging to the Labour movement in Scotland than in any other part of the UK. With the Labour Party weak in Scotland and the ILP cut adrift after 1932, the Labour Party in Britain as a whole became anglo-centric to a degree it could not have afforded to be before. Johnston, firmly based in Scotland in charge of a newspaper past its peak of influence, suffered accordingly.

Johnston's reluctance to leave his Scottish base or to be diverted from his set of Scottish activities, meant that he also played no role in the southern-based policy and research groups set up after the 1931 crisis. Such groups included the New Fabian Research Bureau (NFRB) which was concerned with the kind of financial questions Johnston raised in *Forward* and his other outlets. Through such groups Dalton, Gaitskell, Evan Durbin and others shaped Labour policy more directly and decisively than Johnston could. Johnston would undoubtedly have been an asset to such groups with his grasp of the issues, his rigorous reasoning and commonsensical mode of argument. In such company he may well have sharpened his thinking on planning, and viewed in a different light the monetary theories of such people as Douglas and Soddy. Nor did Johnston hold office on the National Executive Committee of the Labour Party, or on its policy committees.

It was a period in which a traumatised Labour Party was wide open to the strong-willed direction of a respected and sharp-minded figure of the calibre of Johnston. Among much else, it could have been made to be more cognisant of its Scottish heritage and character, and the importance of its Scottish dimension. It was a situation pregnant with opportunity; but Johnston chose to stay at home.

The paradox of Scots in the
Labour Party having to stay
South to exert a Scottish
influence.

- The vacuum caused by
lack of Scottish Parliament.

5 Practical steps for peace and in war (1935-1941)

When the General Election came to be fought in November 1935, the Italian aggression against Abyssinia had put the tense international situation to the forefront of British political life. It was a situation which divided the Labour Party into several camps; the majority view in favour of military sanctions as a last resort left various shades of pacifist opinion either alienated or disheartened.

The issue had also led to the resignation of George Lansbury as party leader and his succession, initially on a temporary basis, by Clement Attlee. Johnston had supported Lansbury and had urged him, up until the last moment, not to resign. Lansbury and Johnston were firm friends and allies, although Johnston did not share Lansbury's belief in unilateral disarmament and absolute non-resistance. Johnston instead supported economic and financial sanctions on the part of the League of Nations against aggressor states, in this case Italy, but drew the line at military sanctions. This view in turn differed from that of the Socialist League, the intellectual Left of the Party, which would endorse no sanctions until Socialists controlled the League of Nations. In Johnston's view military sanctions would simply be unnecessary if economic sanctions were properly applied. Brushing aside objections from such as Morrison and Dalton, he linked the prospects of an International Police Force, international disarmament and true collective security with the success of economic sanctions and the continuance of anti-military propaganda. In *Forward* (19 October 1935) Johnston declared: 'For my part, I conceive military war and the preparation for military war to be the suicide of the nations, and I will have no hand or part in its advocacy.'

Johnston fought West Stirlingshire in the election on this strident anti-war platform. His belief that a growing volume of public opinion favoured economic but not military sanctions was confirmed by the result: Johnston triumphed with a majority of nearly 3,000 over his Tory opponent. It was indeed a notable victory, one of the highlights of Labour's partial recovery from their 1931 position. Scotland continued to suffer more severely from the economic crisis, and Johnston probably convinced many that armaments expenditure would preclude money being spent on unemployment. However, there did seem to be a swelling tide of opinion in Britain against military intervention in Europe. Johnston skilfully played on the widespread desire for collective security through the League of Nations, and argued cogently that to engage in a competition in national armaments would be a negation of it. At this juncture, Johnston's 'middle course' on sanctions was arguably more in line with popular feeling than either outright pacifism or the militarist option. However, there was something disingenuous about his refusal to address himself to the question of what should be done in the event of military aggression being waged against a member, or members, of the League of Nations in defiance of economic sanctions. As Morrison replied to him in *Forward* (5 October 1935), the League, in committing itself to going only so far and no further, would display a weakness liable to be exploited.

Johnston's belief that interventionist action could stop successfully at economic sanctions was attacked as naïve by pacifists as well as those in the majority in the Labour Party. Arthur Ponsonby, a pacifist who resigned the Labour leadership of the House of Lords over the issue, pointed out that the conditions necessary for the success of economic sanctions – that they be applied immediately, unanimously and completely – were absent, and that partial sanctions only made a dangerous situation even more so. For Ponsonby, action of the kind advocated by Johnston implied in practice the dispatch of the British fleet to blockade Italy. Johnston repudiated the latter argument and stuck to his belief that economic sanctions – or, as he preferred to call it, an economic boycott – would obviate the need for military action and fuel a moral movement internationally against militarism. To Johnston the alternative to an economic boycott was 'business as usual': even if the boycott was incomplete it was all Britain could do to register protest. Rather than face Ponsonby's uncomfortable question of whether or not an incomplete boycott would actually worsen the situation, Johnston turned the issue into a straightforward one of Britain conniving with Mussolini or keeping her own hands clean. Profiteers who sought to wax fat on a war once again became the main butt of his polemic.[1]

Johnston's feverish reponse to the threat of war in Europe was a product of an increasing optimism about developments in society generally. He feared that the outbreak of war would set back what he saw as very real social and economic progress. Johnston's New Year message to *Forward* readers in 1936 was headlined 'The Best is Yet to Be', and was confident in its prediction that a new age of co-operation and prosperity was at hand.[2] He still believed, true to his earliest ILP days, that socialism was about to supersede capitalism. The Labour Party, he claimed, was organising the 'forces of socialism and goodwill' against a background of profoundly important advances in medical care, diet and living and working conditions. Johnston was particularly enthused by nutritional progress, spurred largely by the work of his compatriot John Boyd Orr whose *Food, Health and Income* (1936) became a seminal enquiry. For Johnston it was a matter of the utmost urgency that war be avoided to allow 'the gathering forces of Democracy and Human Kindness and Sanity' to usher in an 'era of abundance'. In the course of the next four years, such utopian optimism periodically burst through Johnston's agonised deliberations on international relations. Johnston – in true ILP fashion – found it difficult to be unremittingly pragmatic, and the flashes of romanticism, which came as a kind of release, were incandescent.

Johnston, in his journalism and in the House of Commons, kept up a barrage of anti-war propaganda throughout 1936. He opposed any government increase in armaments spending, on the grounds that it was not being accompanied by genuine attempts to move towards the establishment of an international police force or an international tribunal of equity to settle disputes between nations. He also called for a world conference to insist upon all colonies being mandated through the League of Nations, with equal trading privileges for all nations being ensured in these colonies. In response to the rearmament clamour, Johnston revived his 'Socialist War Points' column in *Forward* and disparaged all talk of war with Nazi Germany. Of the League of Nations' failure to stop Mussolini by economic sanctions, Johnston was unrepentant: he put it down to calculations being upset by Mussolini's use of poison gas to secure a quicker victory. The Spanish Civil War found Johnston as strong in support of the Republican cause as the Left in general, although he chose to concentrate his writings on the press coverage of the war and the attempts to rouse Catholic opinion for France than on the question of British intervention, or indeed voluntary aid for the Spanish Government. A trip to the Baltic and Danzig in the autumn of 1936 gave Johnston first-hand evidence of the nature of Nazism. He was suitably appalled by anti-Semitic propaganda, but on his return rather blunted the impact of his report on it by saying that they in Scotland could hardly 'look askance at the theological hatreds of Eastern Europe' when over thirty people had recently suffered injuries at a 'religious' football match between Rangers and Celtic.[3] On the vexed question of the Polish corridor through Germany, Johnston believed that Germany and Poland could be induced to agree to run the corridor by a joint committee with a neutral chairman, Poland to continue to be free to get goods to the seaboard and Germany to be free to have access across the corridor.[4] In spite of what he knew to be the inherently aggressive and authoritarian nature of Nazism, Johnston believed that international disputes involving Germany were open to such reasonable and equitable solutions.

In his reluctance to accept that Germany was the major threat to peace, Johnston was, in effect, an appeaser who followed the line of the Union of Democratic Control (whose meetings he addressed) in choosing to focus more indignantly on the Versailles Treaty as the source of the trouble. He was, in a sense, only echoing what the majority of British people believed, even if that belief was born of fear. The political parties strove to present an image which was at once purposeful and pacifist. To Johnston this represented an opportunity for Labour to undercut the Government, and he was vigorous in his pursuit of this pro paganda objective. When Sir Samuel Hoare asked in what way the Government's policy was less pacifist than that of Labour, Johnston was quick to seize the initative: firstly, he argued, the Government had allowed and encouraged the private manufacture of armaments and of poison gas and chemicals; and, secondly, it had supplied Japan with munitions in their aggressive raid on Manchuria – the first breakaway from the League of Nations ideal.[5] In this case, as in others, Johnston made a propaganda meal out of crumbs.

For all the pacifist sentiment, the rearmament process gathered pace. Johnston responded by trying to show how such ideas as an international police force might work. He envisaged nations contributing aircraft to this police force; and he suggested that each national contingent be housed in the territory of some nation other than their own. Such measures were also to be accompanied by a 'square deal' to all nations in the matter of raw materials, trade and currency. However, for Johnston, there could be no question of postponing arrangements for an inter national police force pending the resolution of such inequities. 'For my part', he wrote in *Forward*(16 January 1937):

> I can see no reason why we should not boldly and persistently declare that there is not and cannot be any security in national armaments: that they are waste and folly, and almost certain to result in war, that therefore we shall not vote for or support national armament, but demand from our Government an immediate declar-ation that it is prepared to contribute its quota to an International Police Force.

This road, in Johnston's view, was the socialist road. However, it did not convince fellow Socialists like Ponsonby who returned to the polemical fray in *Forward* the following week with a range of practical criticisms about who was to command the police force, how it was to be recruited and who was to supply it with arms. For Ponsonby the unanimity the scheme required was all too elusive and the prospects of its collapsing into divided national units all too likely. Johnston's subsequent rejoinder (30 January 1937) was somewhat lofty and facile, and his charge of 'tribalism' (13 February 1937) in relation to Ponsonby unfair. Neither did Johnston's insistence that an international police force could take action against aggressors without affecting innocent civilians, carry conviction. On the other hand, he was justified in pointing to the support the ideas enjoyed internationally, particularly on the part of the Labour Government in New Zealand, a source of much encouragement and inspiration for Johnston, and many other Democratic Socialists, at this time.

In the House of Commons Johnston's angle on the armaments issue was predominantly that of the scourge of the profiteers. He raised questions of prices, profits and speculation in connection with the armament programme, decried the 'Rearmament Vultures', and raised the spectre of the Great War profiteers to charge the public mood. Raising the issue of interest payments upon the new Armaments Loan to the bankers for the credits they created, Johnston argued that the state should create its own credit by converting the Post Office Savings Bank into a fully-fledged state bank. These campaigns, along with a similar one waged on share-pushers, recalled the crusading journalist of twenty years before.

In July 1937 Johnston, along with Attlee and other leading party figures, urged the Parliamentary Labour Party to vote against the military estimates on the grounds that there was no evidence that the Government was hostile to Fascism, that the weapons might be used for Imperialist purposes, and that acquiescence in armaments policy could lead to acquiescence in conscription and loss of civil liberty. The Party Executive's decision went against Johnston, but he agreed to abide by the majority view and abstain from voting against the Estimates. Indeed, Johnston was by now not nearly as uncompromising in his attitude as people such as Emrys Hughes, who had turned *Forward* on to an anti-war course which was to continue through the duration of the war when it came. Johnston's attitude, as shaped by the Japanese incursion into China in August 1937, became one of despair, the sense of war looming closer serving both to inject a frantic note into his arguments and to alert the pragmatist in him to the dangers of maintaining an Adullamite resistance.

II

At a West Stirling Labour Party meeting on 22 May 1937, Johnston announced his intention to resign his parliamentary seat at the next election. He admitted to feeling the strain caused by parliamentary work and his many other duties and obligations. Johnston wanted time to devote himself to writing and research. Shortly before this meeting he had written letters to Emrys Hughes giving vent to his weariness and frustrations. In the first he wrote: 'A miserable, dreary, health damning life this! Would to God I were away from London and like you, getting the wind of the hills'; and, in the second: 'Am hunting the share pusher swindlers . . . International Polis (and try thereby to keep the L.P. from voting for re-armament against Fascism!) digging out material for a History of Kirkintilloch, hunting Lawyers – Judges who seek increases, looking after Scots business, doing my Friendly Society job, dodging the 'flu, and asking myself if I am sane in trying to do it all.'[6] The allusion in this letter to the rearmament issue is ambiguous, but may suggest that Johnston was doubtful about his stance in view of its practical implications.

Clearly, however, he was unhappy with such a cluttered life, the amount of travelling it involved and the lack of time it afforded him for his writing. As committee meetings and speaking engagements multiplied Johnston felt that his chief talents were getting rusty. He envisaged contributing more written pro-paganda to the service of the Labour Party in the form of books and pamphlets, but he also wanted time to write history. His history of Kirkintilloch actually appeared later in 1937, but rather bears the scars of the hectic circumstances of its birth.

Johnston also produced a pamphlet for the Labour Party in 1937: 'Labour's Policy of Food for All'. In it he summarised arguments he regularly employed in parliamentary debates regarding nutrition and health standards, and made full use of the research work of such people as Boyd Orr. As in his speeches and writings on market surpluses in the 1920s and early 1930s, Johnston exposed the logic of capitalist profit-making in its organisation of scarcity of supply rather than abundance. He lambasted the waste inherent in such a system and outlined a food policy which he claimed would be the 'greatest social reform of our age'. In essentials it was a milk marketing scheme to supply milk to the most needy. Johnston suggested that each medical officer of health in the country be authorised to issue dockets to every mother with children under five years of age, and to every sick and nursing mother, that would enable them to go to any registered milk distributor and get all the milk they required at 1s a gallon. He argued that if it paid the Milk Marketing Board to sell milk at 1s a gallon to schools, it would equally pay them to have that milk sold in unlimited quantities to the poor at 1s a gallon. In halving the price of milk to the poor, Johnston argued that the quantity of milk consumed would be increased, and that this would benefit agriculture. For Johnston it was a policy of equating production to consumption and would help fix the level of production by the amount necessary for consumption. What could be done with milk could also be done, Johnston argued, with potatoes and fish. Johnston repeatedly urged the Government to experiment with national dividends where there was a colonial surplus. In this way, he suggested, consumers in the Colonies would at least eat or wear the surpluses off the markets instead of seeing these surpluses destroyed or price levels crashing.

Related to the issue of health standards was of course housing, and much of Johnston's parliamentary time in this period was taken up in tabling amendments to such controversial legislation as the Rent Restrictions Act, and the generally welcomed Housing (Financial Provisions) (Scotland) Bill. In connection with the latter Johnston stressed the need for grants to improve water supplies in Scotland.

From the time of his return to Parliament after the 1935 election, Johnston acted as Labour's spokesman on Scottish affairs. The experience, while in no way diluting his commitment to the British Labour Party, led him once again to the issue of Scottish Home Rule.

III

Scotland's economic problems were acute in the 1930s. The Depression hit her heavy industries severely and unemployment was appreciably higher than the UK average throughout the decade. This was particularly so in the west of the country, where the bulk of the staple industries were situated. These industries, of course, were export-orientated and the protectionist policies pursued by the National Government brought them no relief. Of the new domestic industries protected by tariffs, very few were established in Scotland, where purchasing power was relatively weak. Rearmament brought a revival in the late 1930s to the traditional industrial sector, but in a sense this only strengthened Scotland's dependence on a narrow economic base to her future detriment.

The Scottish Labour movement became increasingly absorbed into the wider British structure in this decade, a parallel development to the process of economic integration. The reorganisation of the Labour Party in Scotland under Arthur Woodburn, after the ILP split in 1932, brought the party closer in line with the movement in Britain as a whole. Trade union organisation in Scotland was weakened by unemployment, industrial decline and emigration to the south; it too moved to a position of greater dependence on the UK movement. More Scottish trade unions became British-based; mergers and amalgamations increased and the centralisation process invariably shifted the centre of gravity southwards. The Scottish Labour movement looked to the state to intervene and provide, whether in its call for new industrial investment in Scotland, or for action to preserve and revive the staple industries in which it had so much of its rank and file support. Scottish Labour saw its chances of success as largely dependent on the muscle it exerted as part of the wider British movement. Moreover, the objective of securing the best possible measure of social security and welfare benefit for the unemployed was another factor in reinforcing identification with the British state. The economic 'safety net' provided by the State, imperfect as it was, was another deterrent against any rash moves to break the union, or even to resist the process of UK integration.

Johnston's views were inevitably shaped by these structural and economic developments. He approached problems of economic renewal from a fundamentally British perspective, and did not quarrel with the notion of the British State as the supreme planning agency. While not directly involved, Johnston was influenced by the central planning thinking emerging from such groups as Political and Economic Planning (PEP) and the Next Five Years' Group. To Johnston this type of thinking was refreshingly unpartisan and commonsensical. However, Johnston was also anxious to promote local democracy, and to guard against the dangers posed to it by too powerful a centralised state. Cognisant as he was of the structural realities outlined above, and of the force of opinion in favour of central planning, Johnston also wanted clearer recognition of Scotland's needs and effective machinery to serve them. In 1937 he served on the Gilmour Committee which called for the transfer to Edinburgh of Scottish government departments, and for the organisation of regional planning. Culturally, he helped found the Saltire Society in 1935, an organisation which, besides promoting the Arts in Scotland, also concerned itself with social and economic reforms, and with planning Scotland's future physical-ecological character.

If sentiment in favour of Scottish Independence was weak in these years, there was nonetheless wide support for greater economic and administrative devolution. There was much enthusiasm for local and regional planning and initiatives from within Scotland to stimulate new industrial development; in addition, there was dissatisfaction at the way Scottish business was carried out at Westminster, and a desire for greater autonomy on issues of purely Scottish interest. Johnston took up these concerns with vigour.

In December 1936 he took part in a broadcast debate with the National Liberal MP Henderson Stewart. Both men agreed that some measure of devolution of the business of Parliament was necessary. Johnston said that Scottish MPs could deal with such services as agriculture, local government, and education, and administer the spending on them as a Scottish Parliament would. He suggested that they could sit in Edinburgh to do it. Devolution and democracy, he argued, were as much in England's interests as Scotland's. On the economic front, Johnston urged that the major Scottish industries be put on to a public utility corporation basis such as the London Transport Corporation.[7]

Johnston expanded on his ideas for devolution in an article in the political periodical, the *Fortnightly*, in October 1937. In this article Johnston, in some contrast to his past declarations, was unequivocal in his dismissal of the 'vague Jacobitism' which sentimentalised Scottish history and shaped a mawkish sense of national identity. He made it plain that there was no economic basis to this sentiment. He pointed to the extent to which both the Labour movement and the business community were organised in a British context, and to the absence of a desire to fundamentally change this state of affairs on the part of both. Johnston's analysis continued in a thoroughly practical – and almost impersonal – vein. He stressed the need to persuade the English and Welsh of the benefits of Scottish devolution. Any proposals in the direction of self-government, Johnston argued, 'must not only be evolutionary, they must be clear, business-like, and evoke the minimum of opposition both in England and in Scotland'.

Johnston's proposals – or 'practical steps' – essentially concerned the more effective use of the machinery of the Scots Grand Committee at Westminster. He suggested that: (1) all second readings of purely Scottish bills be taken in the Scots Grand Committee and not on the floor of the House of Commons; (2) the Scottish Estimates be considered and voted upon in the Scots Grand Committee; and (3) the Scots Grand Committee, in considering the Estimates, should do so at Edinburgh, where local authorities and the general public could be invited to attend the sessions. Johnston also suggested that control of the Scottish Estimates be handed over to the Scots Grand Committee. In this way much more time could be devoted to them than under the existing system. Johnston made much of the inadequacies of this system in relation to the time spent on Scottish business, citing the fact that, in 1937, agriculture, education and other vital matters got no parliamentary time because of the time taken up by priority issues of housing and health. He pointed to the increasing amount of functions and business taken on by parliament, the impossible burden of work falling on the Scottish Secretary of State, and the consequent assumption of control of Scottish affairs by a civil service bureaucracy. In Johnston's view, this sense of being governed by faceless bureaucrats 400 miles away was the nub of the frustrations and alienation felt by so many Scots.

Johnston argued that Scottish legislation should be a matter during the Committee stages for determination by the Scottish members alone. There was no case, he said, for weighting the Government majority in the Scots Grand Committee; and, in the event of the Government being in a minority among Scottish members, 'it ought not to attempt legislation solely affecting Scotland and opposed to the wishes of her elected representatives'. Johnston also saw no reason why the Scots Grand Committee could not take the second reading of Scottish Bills in addition to the Estimates and Committee stages of these Bills. As he summed it up:

> The important point at the moment is to get the Second Reading
> and the Committee stages on Scottish Bills discussed and voted
> upon by Scots representatives and by Scots representatives alone.
> In my view that is the immediately practical step and it would be
> one on the road to devolution and Home Rule: moreover, it does
> not raise in the English mind difficulties and apprehensions which
> are clearly involved in any proposals for a separate Parliament.

Finally, Johnston repeated his call for the Scots Grand Committee
to sit in Edinburgh. This would be more than a concession to
sentiment, he argued; it would promote greater knowledge of
and interest in the administration, and bring the governors nearer
to the governed.

Johnston took the first step in his campaign of 'persuasion'
by selling these proposals to the Labour Party, and impressing
upon the English Labour MPs the shortcomings in the way Scottish affairs were dealt with. He also sought to assuage apprehen-
sions about Nationalism, a doctrine viewed suspiciously in the
light of the rise of Fascism in Europe. For Johnston there was
nothing to fear provided the economic basis was right and that
Home Rule or devolution developed along socialist lines.[8] It was
a reflection of Johnston's standing in the Labour Party that he
won positive backing on the issue from Attlee, Morrison and
Dalton. In 1937 the London Scots Self-Government Committee
was set up with Johnston as President. This group was closely
associated with the Labour Party and attempted to reconcile
devolutionary proposals such as Johnston's with the Labour
Party's concept of a planned economy.[9] For a brief period there
appeared to be a significant movement towards these goals,
enough to persuade some radical nationalist figures, such as W.
Oliver Brown, that the Labour Party, and not the Scottish
Nationalist Party, was the vehicle for progress in this respect.[10]

Separatist notions and anti-English propaganda were relegated firmly to the margins of Scottish political life, but devolution of Johnston's administrative sort gained momentum. In the short term it was to be overtaken by world events, but the relevance of the administrative and economic devolution approach was before long to be demonstrated by Johnston himself.

IV

As international events grew forbiddingly bleak, and united and popular fronts disintegrated,[11] Johnston continued to fight his corner in the Labour Party for what he called 'the Economic Boycott School'. In the course of 1938, however, his tone gradually sharpened against the Nazi menace, and ambivalence crept into his outlook. As preparations started to be made for civil defence, Johnston found it difficult to condemn such action as warlike, as Hughes did in *Forward*. Munich reinforced the heavy sense of dilemma. Johnston wrote:

> I confess I find it difficult to clarify my emotions about the events of last weekend. Relief, almost gratitude, that our generation has had another escape – however temporary – from war. Shame and humiliation at the way the Czechs were egged on and 'guaranteed', and then left in the lurch! And finally apprehension that every ally we abandon, every friend we betray, leaves us the weaker for the day when the goose-stepping gangsters will order us in turn to put up our hands.[12]

It was not long before Johnston concluded that something had to be done in self-defence.

Thus in March 1939, in the House of Commons, he gave support to the measures of civil defence, including air-raid precautions. This was something of a wrench for Johnston, but he could not in all conscience opt out of the social effort necessary to protect himself and his fellow citizens. After a solemn and

sorrowful speech about 'bleak and dismal international relationships' and the 'sense of hush before a storm', Johnston addressed
himself to what he saw as the inadequacies of food and water
supplies and the evacuation procedures. It was a turning point;
Johnston had in effect advertised his suitability for engaging in
what was inescapably war work of a kind.[13]

It did not, however, mark the end of his quest for possible
means of avoiding war. Although increasingly pessimistic,
Johnston continued to advance ideas deserving of notice. In *Forward* and in the *Fortnightly* he suggested: internationalising the
Suez canal and Gibraltar, and internationalising the colonial
dependencies of the nations who ruled Africa. Peace and security,
he argued, would be more likely if the world powers shared
ownerships and responsibilities and became equal heritors in the
world estate. In relation to the first proposal, Johnston believed
that internationalising such crucial strategic territories would
herald a real collective security effort which Britain, as the con-
trolling power of these territories, could begin. As for the colonies,
Johnston claimed that a trade boom would open up for all as
the African millions were organised in new markets with
increased spending power for goods. It was an idea redolent of
Johnston's empire schemes of the 1920s and early 1930s. There
could be no collective security, Johnston argued, while there
were 'have' and 'have not' nations; hence the proposal of international ownership of great highways and colonial empires.[14]

Neither did Johnston look more kindly on conscription. He
believed that it would be useless as a military weapon, and feared
that it could be used as a weapon against the working class.
Conscription, for Johnston and the Labour Party, did not mean
equality of sacrifice. He did not believe, however, that Labour
councils should protest against conscription by refusing to take
civil defence action. Moreover, Johnston was adamant that such
preparations were non-military, a view which was derided by

Labour and left-wing opponents of the measures. Johnston saw a clear distinction between measures to protect civilians, and armed preparations to fight.

Indeed, by May 1939, Johnston had become involved at government level in civil defence. He had been invited, shortly after his House of Commons speech in support of such preparations, to become Regional Commissioner for Civil Defence in Scotland. Johnston later claimed that fear of being implicated in another Munich made him stall – he agreed to co-operate in making the necessary arrangements but reserved his decision about formal acceptance of the post until, and if, the country should actually be at war.[15]

Johnston worked initially with the Lord Advocate (T. M. Cooper). The whole civil defence operation at this time was presided over by Sir John Anderson (then Lord Privy Seal), of whose administrative and executive talents Johnston was respectful. There was much to be done: in May Johnston and Cooper reported on the inadequacy of evacuation plans in Scotland concerning the redirection of food supplies from partly depopulated vulnerable areas to the reception areas where the population would have multiplied, and on the deficiencies in water supplies to reception areas. Johnson was also concerned at the lack of green vegetables being grown in Scottish gardens, and the escalation of the prices of air-raid shelters.[16] Johnston made much of matters regarding profiteering and price-ramping of necessary defence materials at the regional commissioners' meetings. In accelerating civil defence procedures, Johnston had to work closely with local authorities and to chase up those who were being neglectful. For a time Scottish air-raid precautions, particularly in Glasgow, were woefully inadequate, and Johnston's relations with Patrick Dollan, now Glasgow Lord Provost, became strained.

On 26 August 1939 Johnston was officially appointed Regional

Commissioner for Scotland. A week later war was declared. As late as July, Johnston had still clung to faint hopes that the internationalisation of colonial empires and world peace conferences could avert war.[17] Now he dwelt no longer on pipe-dreams, but turned his practical expertise wholeheartedly to war work. The position of Regional Commissioner gave him wide scope for his energies. Besides the range of administrative and co-ordinating responsibilities, the post carried with it the power to act as the sole civil authority in the event of communications being cut with the central government in war. Talk of 'dictators' was frequently heard, and tact had to be employed to give the lie to such taints. Johnston was assisted by Lord Airlie – a Conservative – and the District Commissioners of the five districts into which Scotland was divided. On the outbreak of war, Johnston stressed that although he was prepared to participate in the administrative effort, he was against the Labour Party joining the Government. He believed that a coalition, as in the past, would end in humiliation for the Labour Party representatives. Some Labour MPs viewed even the Regional Commissioner role with suspicion, and Johnston found himself pushed off the Parliamentary Executive in November, on the grounds that his new post had left him little time to attend Parliament.

Johnston found much to perturb his sense of propriety and efficiency in his civil defence work. On 11 September 1939 he wrote to Anderson about the system of 'standing armies' of paid wardens, auxiliary firemen, first-aid parties and so on. He pointed out that many were drawing a wage for doing nothing, something that was demoralising both to themselves and to those who volunteered; that these paid men were the only class of men giving no voluntary service whatsoever; and that consideration should be given as to whether only a skeleton staff of auxiliary firemen and ARP wardens should be maintained, the rest being absorbed back into industrial production. Johnston was very keen that more be done by voluntary service and he held up the example of the town of Ayr, which organised completely on a part-time or voluntary service basis.[18] Anderson, impressed by a kindred administrator's holistic bent, duly followed up these points.

Johnston was much preoccupied in maintaining civilian morale. His reassurances about equality across the board in rationing, and his personal war on profiteering helped to infuse an egalitarian spirit of equality of sacrifice which was as prominent in Scotland as in the rest of Britain from the early stages of the war. In keeping with this spirit, Johnston, in December 1939, alluded to the question of credit inflation resulting from the defence loan, and reiterated his suggestion that credits created for the war be created in the name of the Prime Minister and Chancellor of the Exchequer, acting for the nation. This, said Johnston, would ensure that the country would not in the future be paying unnecessary dividends and interest upon inflated credit, but instead paying the interest on credit created by themselves into their own national account. The country, argued Johnston, had to prevent a repetition of the inflationary processes which proved so damaging in the last war.[19] On this issue his advice was ignored.

The Regional Commissioner post afforded Johnston many opportunities to pursue personal hobby-horses, especially in relation to marketing schemes for foodstuffs; and it brought out his ingeniously resourceful use of disparate assets. As Hugh Dalton recorded in his diary after meeting Johnston in December 1939, Johnston had 'solved the problem of the forests' by offering 3d a pound for all venison delivered in fit condition to be turned into venison sausages. These sausages were cheaper and popular with the public. This kind of imaginative and practical resourcefulness epitomised Johnston, and he clearly revelled in it. Dalton wrote of him: 'He is thoroughly enjoying his job as Regional

Prescient points.

Commissioner and potential dictator, for Scotland, and, I judge, doing it very well.'[20]

With tragic prescience Johnston urged the Scottish people in 1940 and early 1941 to become more 'blitz-minded'. He said that thousands of more voluntary fire-fighters were needed and stressed the folly of relying solely on the fire brigade. 'It is a greater act of civil defence', he stated, 'to extinguish an incendiary bomb than to burrow in a shelter. But, alas, in Scotland the average citizen is still far from being fire- conscious or aware that it is his or her urgent duty to equip himself or herself individually, and in concert with neighbours, to deal timeously with the incendiary bomb.' Criticism was also levelled by Johnston at those business firms who were intent on finding legal loopholes by which they could escape from providing fire-watchers. Even the churches felt Johnston's wrath on this matter; they were guilty, he said, of displaying a similar lack of urgency. Johnston had in fact come to the view that a limited form of civil defence conscription was now desirable.[21] This did not go down well in general, and there was also press criticism of Johnston's fire-fighting appeal: this did not take enough account of local conditions and problems, wrote one leader-writer, and people were not clear as to what was expected of them. Moreover, the view was held that Johnston had not answered important questions concerning fire-fighting in tenements and the practical difficulties that were posed.[22]

However, such criticism was rare, and Johnston was probably right in thinking that people had, by the beginning of 1941, come to value the regional organisation. He was indeed hopeful that some of its functions would become a permanent feature of the local government system.[23] He had, in a short time, obtained an impressive degree of voluntary effort and efficient administration with relatively little resort to compulsion.

His impact on government circles had also been favourable.

The coalition headed by Churchill had been in power since May 1940. From the end of that year Churchill had been planning cabinet moves and had canvassed Johnston about coming into the Government. Minister of Health was one post dangled before him, but Johnston insisted that he was doing more useful work as Regional Commissioner. Churchill, however, was persistent. He knew that with a Labour stalwart like Johnston in the Scottish Office the prospects of another 'Red Clyde' disruption of war production were remote. On hearing of Johnston's desire to write history, Churchill urged him to make it instead. After much hesitation, Johnston was swayed by the offer of the Secretaryship for Scotland.[24] The appointment dated from 9 February 1941.

6 *Scots wha hae (1941-1965)*

Johnston fully recognised the extent of the opportunity the Scottish Office presented. Since 1939, following the recommendations of the Gilmour Committee, Scottish government departments, newly rationalised, had been situated in Edinburgh, at St Andrews House. This was now the administrative power-house. Very little government business was left at Whitehall. As an historian of the Scottish Office has pointed out, the new system was a flexible one: 'The Secretary of State for Scotland was now an overlord over an empire whose character could be changed from time to time by administrative fiat.' There now existed a structure 'that could easily become overnight a Home Rule adminsitration'.[1]

Johnston was to prove himself adept at manipulating the new structures. He struck up sound working relationships with his civil servants, for whom his clarity of purpose and straightforward decisiveness were welcome ministerial traits. He exploited the strong *esprit de corps* which quickly built up among administrators in Edinburgh, determined not to be mere functionaries of Whitehall mandarins. Johnston was also well supported by two Under-Secretaries, an innovation of wartime designed to provide political balance. Joseph Westwood (Labour) was one, Col. Scryngemour Wedderburn (later replaced by Allan Chapman) was his Conservative collegue. For the position of Parliamentary Private Secretary, Johnston chose Arthur Woodburn, whose administrative capabilities he knew well. All in all it was a solid team which worked smoothly under Johnston's confident leadership.

Shrewdly, Johnston did not accept Churchill's offer without setting conditions. The first was that he would forego his ministerial salary (Johnston had also refused to accept his Regional Commissioner's salary). The second was his master-stroke: that he would form a Council of the living ex-secretaries of State for Scotland to consider Scottish issues, and that when they were unanimous about a course of action to follow, he would expect the Cabinet to give him their backing. This Council of Ministers, dubbed by the press 'The Council of State', represented, as Professor Harvie has said, 'a sort of Scottish equivalent to the coalition cabinet'.[2] Its significance lay in the way that it provided Johnston with cross-party political backing to expedite his legislative and administrative programme, and in satisfying public opinion in Scotland that Scottish interests were being pursued more vigorously, and with more tangible results, than before.

Johnston's commitment to Scotland's best interests was absolute, and this conveyed itself to the people. Few politicans can have made such an instant and profound impact on the popular consciousness as someone to be trusted. He was only months in office when Will Y. Darling, Lord Provost of Edinburgh and an important associate of Johnston's in wartime, wrote of him: 'The propagandist idealist applies his ideas to his task. It is not easy. He has his discouragements but he has united Scottish public opinion most successfully. He impresses me as a man who has got everything he wants for himself. He isn't after anything except Scotland, and for its welfare, betterment, progress he would give all.'[3]

Johnston knew he had the chance to demonstrate that Scotland could take care of its own affairs to the benefit of the whole United Kingdom. He aimed to show the rest of the British people, and not least the Scots themselves, that Home Rule was more efficient. His approach was in the spirit of his devolutionary programme of 1937. Replying in a letter, in August 1942, to the veteran Nationalist Roland Muirhead who had expressed the view that plans for Scottish reconstruction were 'fatuous' without self-government, Johnston declared that he intended in the existing circumstances to keep Scotland 'on the map' and 'to persuade Scots and English alike that it is desirable we *should* be allowed to work out our own problems in our own way'.[4] Johnston was intent on preparing Scotland for the post-war era on its own terms: 'Collaboration with England is one thing', he stated early in 1942, 'absorption is another.'[5] His was a fervent patriotism directed at practicabilities and the milking of opportunities. Johnston was the archetypal Scotsman 'on the make' during the war – purely for Scotland.

II

The Council of State was convened by September 1941. It compromised the following ex-Secretaries of State as well as Johnston himself: Lord Alness (formerly Robert Munro), Sir John Colville, Sir Archibald Sinclair, Ernest Brown, and Walter Elliot. Dismissing the prophecies of Maxton and McGovern of the ILP that he would become a prisoner of these Conservatives and Liberals, Johnston stressed that the Council would assume a non-partisan political character pledged to foster national unity. This was precisely the kind of consensual context he had sought to operate in for many years. When announcing the Council's establishment in the House of Commons, Johnston stated that it would survey Scottish problems of reconstruction and select personnel to undertake inquiries into them. The Council itself was not to participate in the inquiries. Johnston explained that if the Council were agreed on the reports of these Committees of Inquiry, then speedy implementation either of legislation or of administrative action would follow. The Council held its first meeting on 29 September and agreed to institute inquiries into the further development of hydro-electricity in Scotland, the herring industry, and hill sheep farming.[6] These were to be the first of the thirty-two inquiries set up by the Council in the course of the war.

Johnston was also involved, soon after taking office, in planning for reconstruction in Britain as a whole. He, Ernest Brown (Minister of Health) and Lord Reith (Minister of Works) formed a Council of Ministers to co-ordinate the work of future town and country planning. These ministers had to ensure that the administration of the Town and Country Planning Acts and any legislation implementing the recommendations of the Uthwatt Committee on land to be acquired for post-war building should proceed in conformity with long-term planning policy, as it was progressively developed. Johnston insisted that his Council of State would not come into conflict with this long-term planning work, but the Council's existence strengthened his hand in his negotiations with Reith (also a Scot) to ensure that Scotland kept her future planning in her own hands.[7] Johnston's technique was simple: the council was in existence and had agreed on certain courses of action – therefore it would be difficult, if not impossible, to go back on these decisions. This was the kind of *fait accompli* tactic he used in cabinet and in dealings with other ministers and committees to great effect. The case of planning powers illustrated this method of successful manouevring: these were fully rested with the Secretary of State for Scotland while the Minister of Works took control of England and Wales. Johnston then later used his powers to set up planning groups for the major Scottish regions.

At its third meeting on 8 December 1941, the Council of State turned its attention on the vulnerable state of Scottish industry, a topic at the top of Johnston's list of priorities. At an earlier meeting, the desirability of attracting new war industries to Scotland and retaining them after the war on other work was expressed.[8] Now the Council made clear its concern that the industrial trends seemed to be in the other direction. Anxiety was expressed regarding the Government's policy of concentration of industry, and Johnston was given the backing of the Council to report this disquietude to the President of the Board of Trade (Hugh Dalton). Johnston was to make clear the Council's concern regarding the withdrawal of ancillary industries from Scotland, contrary to the policy of attracting lighter industries, and also at the fact that the expansion of industry in Scotland was ephemeral, being almost entirely confined to munitions and war industries which would decline rapidly after hostilities ceased, while more permanent industries were attracted to England.[9]

At the Council's next meeting Johnston came up with the idea of forming a new body for the express purpose of safeguarding Scottish industry and attracting new industrial concerns. He suggested that local authority associations be induced to co-operate with the Scottish Development Council to form the nucleus of his new body, which could in turn be augmented by businessmen and trade unionists. The result, in Johnston's view, would be 'an Industrial Committee or Council which could keep a watch on war-time industrial developments from the point of view of post-war requirements in Scotland and advise the Scottish Council on post-war problems on questions of industrial development and location as affecting Scotland'.[10]

Consequently, a 'Council on Industry' came into being in February 1942. It emerged out of a conference convened by Johnston and attended by representatives of the Chamber of Commerce, the STUC, the Scottish Development Council, the local authorities, and government departments. Getting these people together was a *coup* in itself; organising them speedily into action was remarkable. But the Council on Industry, chaired by Will Y. Darling with Sir Steven Bilsland (an industrialist) as his deputy, buckled to its task with the appropriate sense of urgency and the by now customary wartime spirit of collective endeavour. For Johnston, 'the stage was now set for all possible preventive action to stop, save in cases where good cause was shown, the drift south of industry, particularly peace-time industries. It was of the utmost importance that timeous information should be obtained both of proposed movements of industry out of Scotland and of the establishment of new industries throughout the country.' The other members of the Council of State were suitably impressed by Johnston's initiative.[11]

In fact, it was not long before it became clear that Johnston had struck on a winning formula. By the end of 1942 Scotland's industrial condition was decidedly healthier. Factory space used simply for storage was increasingly turned over to production (Johnston took delight in regularly announcing the statistical evidence, in square feet, of the changes), fewer workers (especially females) were forced to go south for employment, new industries such as childrens' outerwear, uniform clothing, utility clothing, bedding, and linoleum were attracted. Unemployment fell to under 20,000 from 200,000 at the start of the war. From 1942 to the end of the war some 700 new enterprises or substantial extensions were set up in Scotland.

Johnston worked closely with the Council on Industry. The Council would collect the relevant facts about industries which proposed to leave Scotland or industries which might be attracted to it. Johnston then put these facts before the Council of State, and with its backing proceeded to fight the case for Scotland, either to stop industries leaving or to bring others in, with the Ministers of the Production departments, particularly at the Board of Trade. In this Johnston was indefatigable. No industrial objective in Scotland's interests was too trifling or too insignificant to pursue. No means of getting Scotland a fair share of industrial production was left unexplored.

Thus, *inter alia*, he prevented the departure of the pottery industry to England, and the transfer of a major part of Scotland's textile industry to Northern Ireland; he won a share of government printing orders of Post Office directories for the printing industry; he had Scottish firms placed on government lists so that they were eligible to tender for government contracts; he persuaded the Ministry of Aircraft Production to locate more new projects in Scotland; he fought a campaign for greater equalisation of freight charges throughout the UK; he managed to re-open English markets which had been closed to Scottish agricultural surpluses; and he generally impressed Whitehall with the unity of vested interests and opinion which he had adroitly pulled together. As early as May 1942 the *Glasgow Herald*, in common with the rest of the Scottish press, was crediting Johnston with the reversal of the 'drift south' and the redress of the imbalance of war industry location.[12] The press were entirely correct: this was a veritable personal triumph on Johnston's part. His energy, ingenuity, persistence and organising skill were never better displayed, while his Councils of State and of Industry were probably the most effective pressure groups in wartime Britian. In his St Andrew's Day message in 1942, Johnston made it clear that in his view the improvements were the result of curbing partisan political strife and of widening the areas of co-operation and mutual aid.[13] At this juncture unity of purpose was at a peak in Scotland and Johnston was indubitably its alchemist.

III

Johnston's achievement in other areas was more ambiguous. A new hydro-electricity scheme for the Scottish Highlands became a reality: a personal success for Johnston in the short term if not quite the invaluable national asset he hoped it would later become. The Committee of Inquiry, chaired by the Lord Justice Clerk, Lord Cooper, reported late in 1942 and delivered the recommendation Johnston wanted. He then wasted no time in pushing through the required legislation without a division in the early part of 1943. As Johnston explained to the Commons, the Bill provided for a public services corporation, operating on a non-profit basis, harnessing the water power of the North of Scotland, opening up the Highlands to new industries and providing employment, he estimated, for about 10,000 men for ten years. Objections regarding the harm that might be done to the natural beauties of the Highlands, and from landowners anxious about their game reserves, Johnston swept aside. Again the impressive show of unity behind him steamrollered the measure to the Statute Books, and Johnston later ensured that the Board did not have any of its powers as established by the Act curtailed by the Central Generating Board. All this further enhanced Johnston's reputation and popularity. This was all the more pronounced in that it relieved the frustrations of the Scottish public over the delays and hindrances which had bedevilled previous attempts to electrify the Highlands. To Johnston it was an important part of his dream – held since his earliest political days – of re-establishing a self-supporting population in the Highlands and seeing the renaissance of the heart of 'Scotia'.[14] It was a dream never to be truly realised.

Johnston also had grand designs for Scottish education. Having set up a substitute Home Rule 'cabinet' and a 'Parliament on Industry', he proceeded, in November 1942, to establish a 'Parliament on Education'.[15] This was in the form of an Advisory Council consisting of representatives of education, politics and industry. Its overriding object was to consider the whole question of educational reform in post-war Scotland. More specifically, Johnston initially gave the Advisory Council five remits in order of priority: first came the teaching of citizenship in Scottish schools, followed by the organisation and curricula of primary and nursery schools, the organisation and curricula of secondary schools with reference to the award of the Junior and Senior leaving Certificates, technical education, and the recruitment and training of teachers. This proved to be too ambitious a pro-gramme, and the Council was soon instructed to concentrate on four issues: citizenship, primary education, secondary education, and the recruitment of teachers. After reports had been submitted on these, Johnston issued new remits, in November 1943, on teacher training and technical education. Further reports were also submitted by the end of 1944 on adult education grants and education authority bursaries.

An Education (Scotland) Bill was introduced early in 1945, the Scottish equivalent of the Butler Act for England and Wales. The Bill provided for the raising of the school-leaving age, insti-tuted secondary education as a compulsory stage in the educa-tional process, and provided for adult education. However, Johnston stressed that the Bill differed from the Butler Act in its deliberate avoidance of the religious question, and the provi-sion for greater devolution of powers to local authorities and local Education Committees.[16] Johnston believed that the Bill bore the impress of his Advisory Council, but his claims in this regard have been qualified by educationalists.[17]

The Bill did not, however, enshrine Johnston's cherished con-cept of citizenship teaching or his desire to see school curricula pay more attention to applied and domestic science and less to what he considered to be rather recondite subjects such as classics (he himself had undergone a classically-biased schooling and plainly considered it of questionable value). His failure in relation to citizenship affected him most, as is evident in his memoirs.[18] He viewed citizenship teaching as a powerful antidote to the problem of juvenile delinquency, a phenomenon which alarmed Johnston in its apparent wartime increase. Moreover, he believed that citizenship was the very key to a healthy educational system: 'If the purpose and spirit of our educational machine are right, if the object is to fit future generations to live cleanly and worthily in mutual aid and social service, then all else will come right'.

School pupils, Johnston stressed, needed to be taught to think for themselves *and* to think of others.[19] Johnston tried to infuse Scottish education with a truly democratic and collectivist spirit, but, impressive as the energy and dedication of his Advisory Council was on his behalf, he came up against entrenched bureaucratic obstacles in the Scottish Education Department, and tenaciously traditional values and concepts. His progress in this sphere was consequently limited.

Housing was a matter of extreme urgency during the war. With the backing of the Council of State, Johnston reconstituted the Scottish Housing Advisory Committee in May 1942. Sub-committees were then set up to deal with such issues as housing design, regional distribution of housing, provision of housing by private enterprise, and rural housing. Of the members of the Council of State it was Walter Elliot who took most to do with housing, and who brought his own experience of housing problems in the 1936-38 period of his Secretaryship to bear on the wartime situation. Elliot had a firm grasp of the complex of difficulties which housing programmes involved. Chief of these was the supply of labour, and Johnston fought successfully in cabinet to meet Scottish needs in this respect. In December 1943 he stressed the urgent need for further labour for repair and maintenance work and also for site works necessary in preparation for new housing schemes. He argued that overcrowding in Scotland was far worse than England and that there was greater need for more men to be employed on housing work. He thus suggested that an arrangement be made whereby men of the National Fire Service, while continuing to be members of that service, should be made available for housing work on the understanding that in emergency they would be recalled to the Fire Service. This supply of labour was to be additional to the numbers who were to be released from the Fire Service. The Minister of Labour, Ernest Bevin, duly agreed to this.[20] Johnston, in fact, was given consistent cabinet backing for his building programmes and the contingency measures he was forced to adopt to undertake them.

Johnston introduced a Housing Bill for Scotland in September 1944. Its main provision was to extend the open subsidy for general needs, so that money could be diverted from purely slum clearance and overcrowding problems, to permit the Government to provide houses for young couples who did not come under either the category of slum clearance or of overcrowding. It was a bill also designed to get round obstructions and delays which frequently accompanied matters such as the surveying and servicing of sites. Private house-building was given encouragement as well as local authority building. Damage and destruction inflicted during air-raids did of course make Johnston's task many times more difficult. Johnston's housing targets – he set 30,000 in late 1941 – were rather ambitious, but significant progress, largely through the Scottish Housing Advisory Committee, was made in the preliminary work necessary in connection with sites. The groundwork at least was well laid for a major post-war building programme.

To assist such a programme, Johnston ensured that the separate Town and County Planning Bill for Scotland should address itself chiefly to the special problems of the blitzed areas. The Bill provided for the acquisition of derelict land and faciliated the task of land clearance. Johnston was also proud to state in the Commons that, unlike its English counterpart, the Bill imposed the minimum control on local planning authorities and encouraged voluntary co-operation between them.[21] On the important issue of planning therefore, Johnston consistently worked for decentralised control and increased clout for regional planning associations. This flowed from his initial stance in favour of separate Scottish planning powers and against absorption with England and – effectively – Whitehall. In relation to the reconstitution of the Forestry Commission, Johnston also fought for a separate

Scottish structure. In this he was only partly successful: in the event there was only one Forestry Commission, but there was provision for a separate Scottish Committee of which Johnston was to become Chairman after the war. Scottish agricultural and fishing interests were pursued vigorously by Johnston in cabinet; he fought unsuccessfully to fix milk prices, but he did manage to guarantee important markets, to boost home consumption of products such as herring, and to place post-war expansion in both industries on the agenda. Government support was also secured for a scheme to develop the Clyde Valley Region. Johnston did not forget the tourist industry either, forming a Scots Ancestry Research Council and paving the way for the establishment of a Scottish Tourist Board.

One clear failure in Johnston's record concerned his attempt to get the Scottish MPs to meet regularly in Edinburgh, another throwback to his 1937 proposals. Only twenty seven actually showed up at the first meeting in October 1941, and Johnston quickly abandoned the idea as a lost cause. It hardly mattered, for Johnston, by other means aforementioned, was able to convince the Scottish people in general that Scotland was being listened to and was receiving her due.

Nonetheless, Johnston was not entirely dismayed by signs of nationalist activity, for he found that he could turn them to advantage in the Cabinet. Here he used the threat of nationalist unrest as a bargaining tool as Herbert Morrison has recalled in his memoirs.[22] However, it does seem that Johnston interpreted the relatively strong wartime electoral showings by the Scottish National Party, as an indication of the beginnings of a Scottish 'Sinn Fein' movement.[23] This he regarded with a jaundiced eye; he saw such a movement as a wrecking force to his constructive form of administration, and to the erection of sound economic foundations for future Scottish prosperity.

IV

Apart from specifically Scottish issues, Johnston made a notable contribution to government deliberations on a National Health service scheme. From late 1943 till the end of the war he worked closely with the Minister of Health, Henry Willink, in tackling the formidable difficulties the scheme faced. Following the Beveridge Report late in 1942, the Government agreed in principle that there should be a comprehensive health service available to all. However, settling the practical details to the satisfaction of the politicans and the interest groups involved proved to be a Herculean task.

Johnston's input to a government discussions was all the more significant for the success of his Scottish public health policies. In particular, the Clyde Basin Experiment reflected great credit upon him. This concerned Johnston's decision to extend the facilities of civil defence hospitals in the Clyde valley to civilian war workers. Under Johnston's scheme, patients on the waiting lists of voluntary hospitals were admitted to the new hosptials built for the Emergency Medical Service. By February 1944, Johnston claimed that 26,000 patients had been dealt with in this way and that the voluntary hospitals had co-operated in making the scheme a success. So successful was it, in fact, that it was soon extended to the rest of Scotland and became known as the Supplementary Medical service or the 'Emergency Hospital Scheme'. In accordance with this scheme general practitioners were able to refer any patients for whom they felt that specialist advice was desirable to the Regional Medical Officers of the Department of Health and, through them, to consultants in private practice. No fees were charged, and Johnston won the full support of the consultants to the arrangement.[24] These were outstanding administrative achievements on Johnston's part, and they lent weight to his attempts in cabinet, and in the Government's committee for post-war reconstruction, to bring about a UK-wide service along Beveridge lines.

Johnston's views were largely brought to bear on the draft White Paper he prepared with Willink and presented on 3 January 1944.[25] This paper solidly recommended free medical treatment for all and state control over the distribution of doctors in the public service. The preservation of private practice, the main concern of the Conservative Willink, was also assured. However, Johnston and Willink oc021d not come to agreement on the issue of whether hospitals should recover maintenance charges from their patients. Willink took the view that voluntary hospitals could not survive without this. Johnston disagreed and claimed that voluntary hospital opinion in Scotland was against a charge. He argued, in the Reconstruction Committee, that a means test in respect of cost of maintenance would be the worst possible start for the new hospital service. In Johnston's opinion it would be preferable to raise the Social Security contribution payable by employers and employed so as to cover the full cost. The general feeling of the Committee was in support of Johnston,[26] and maintenance charges were not included in the final version of the White Paper.[27] Johnston, unlike Attlee, agreed with Willink's view that the best doctors would not be attracted into the public service unless they were also allowed to take private patients. Johnston and Willink were well aware of the importance of securing the co-operation of the medical profession, and of the opposition they were likely to face. However, both were confident that over ninety per cent of the population would use the public service,[28] a prediction which was proved accurate when the service was eventually introduced in 1948. Johnston had less trouble reaching agreement with the Scottish doctors than Willink did with the English ones, and he also managed – in another bravura display of administrative finesse – to get agreement between local authorities, voluntary hospitals and Regional Hospitals Councils.[29] All this was at least partly the result of Johnston's insistence on separate Scottish administration of the general practitioner service and the administration of hospitals by the major Scottish local authorities.[30]

Johnston and Willink also got through a power of cabinet work on housing. Some of this went in tandem with Johnston's policies for Scotland, but much of it was central to the shaping of post-war programmes for Britain as a whole. In cabinet and in the Reconstruction Committee, Johnston and Willink fought successfully against any reduction in the proposed labour force for the building industry or any alteration to the apprenticeship training scheme in the industry as set out in the White Paper of 1943. The government, they urged, should not refrain from announcing that the contemplated labour force in the building industry would be $1\frac{1}{4}$ million.[31] Johnston and Willink also urged the Government to approve emergency factory-made houses out of steel and timber, and to allow them to open discussions with local authorities on the vexed questions of acquiring sites and preparing them.[32] A 'mass attack' on the housing problem could not, in Johnston and Willink's estimation, be delayed.

In his firm and passionate struggle to press on with such 'grand designs' in housing, health and other areas of social policy, Johnston was an archetypal apostle of 'New Jerusalem'. Johnston's cabinet position prevented his siding with those, in the House of Commons Debate, who considered the government too tepid in its response to Beveridge. However, he was clearly one of those in government who were determined to seize on the chance provided by the country's wartime mood in favour of the Report and post-war reconstruction on a massive scale.

In the view of Corelli Barnett,[33] those, like Johnston, who advanced the cause of 'New Jerusalem' simply avoided confronting the fundamental economic difficulties and chose to put their ethics and ideals before resources. Rather than make the reconstruction of Britain's industrial base their priority, the 'New Jerusalemers' focused on social welfare, to the nation's future economic detriment. For Barnett, the typical 'New Jerusalemer' was one who had resisted rearmament and clung to a utopian vision of a world saved from conflict through disarmament and the League of Nations; one whose social vision prevented appreciation of the need to revitalise industry and train the nation to meet the future technological challenges.

Johnston certainly fits into the first part of Barnett's characterisation of the 'New Jerusalemer'. However, it would certainly be unfair to Johnston to accuse him of having anything less than an acute appreciation of the importance of industrial renewal, as his efforts on behalf of Scottish industry show. Moreover, Johnston was strongly in favour of increased technical education and training, although this was eclipsed by the teaching of citizenship in his scale of educational priorities. Rather, it would be fairer to say that Johnston linked healthy economic performance to a sound social basis, not the other way round. It was certainly the case that he, like most leading political figures in wartime, had not calculated the costs, but, equally, he was convinced that the losses resulting from passing up the opportunity of a more socially just and secure Britain would be incalculable. To Johnston it was simply unthinkable that such progressive achievements could be forfeited.

With victory in Europe the coalition Government reached its end in May 1945. Back in January, Johnston had reflected pessimistically that peace would bring a return to partisan politics and consequent divisions in society. 'We shall be split into groups and ideologies all scambling for mastery –', he opined, sensing that the mood of co-operation and the unity of purpose was about to pass.[34] He had no desire to be part of party politics again. The end of the coalition was, in effect, the end of Johnston the politician, a role in which he had never been personally happy, notwithstanding his ability, reputation and achievements.

The Scottish press, which he had cultivated – and manipulated – with the journalist's skill, bade him fond farewell with a chorus of grateful praise. Nonetheless, while it hardly intended to sound a dour note, the *Glasgow Herald* perhaps put the credit Johnston was due in its proper perspective and thereby pointed to the real nature of his achievement. The editorial stated: 'He took over at a moment when the national fortunes were approaching the lowest ebb. He departs just as the magnitude of Scottish domestic problems is beginning to be generally understood. It is due largely to his energy, intelligence and patience that these problems are not more numerous or more urgent . . . '.[35]

V

Johnston's achievement, then, was to prevent Scotland's industrial and economic problems from worsening during the war, rather than to resolve them. That was beyond him, and, it might safely be said, anyone else. His accomplishments were many, varied and in some cases spectacular, but they did not constitute the necessary medicine for export industries about to be pitched again to the storms of international competition, or for domestic industries too confined by market forces. In spite of Johnston's achievement in winning Scotland a due share of wartime industrial production, the country's economic base was still debilitatingly narrow after 1945. In strict economic terms, Johnston's was a holding or a salvage operation conducted with dedication, innovation, tenacity and flair. He also offered hope, and the spirit both of enterprise and co-operation which he fostered might have led to economic improvement had it lasted sufficiently far into peacetime.

Of course, the peculiar circumstances of wartime played their part in bringing opportunities for positive action. Johnston was favoured by circumstances which able ex-Secretaries of State such as Walter Elliot might also have exploited with positive results. It is difficult, however, to imagine anyone bettering the use Johnston made of the collaborative spirit of the time and the bi-partisan political context. The Council of State and the Council on Industry were masterly administrative devices and it was fitting that the latter should survive Johnston's departure from office. Through the former Johnston achieved a greater degree of consensus than the Cabinet on issues which were potentially divisive, a consensus, moreover, which was decidely more left of centre, notwithstanding the fact that Johnston was the Council's only Labour member. The Council of State, for example, backed Johnston's extension of emergency medical services to civilians, and agreed with his view that 'the retention of state medical and hospital services in Scotland should command the support of all political parties'.[36] This was, of course, in advance of the National Health Service, over which there were significant disagreements between government ministers.

Johnston's talents were ideally suited to the atmosphere of experimentation and the relative openness of wartime government. He was at his best in co-ordinating the efforts of experts who were freed from 'compartmentalism': trade unionist worked with industrialist and engineer spoke to architect. Johnston fused their respective talents and also spurred them to creative action beyond the bounds of their own fields. His importance as a catalyst in these respects can hardly be over-stressed. Such freedom of scope for quick and positive action would not be the norm in peacetime, and this was probably the main reason why Johnston decided against continuing in politics after 1945.

That Johnston was a success – the most successful indeed of Scottish Secretaries of State – has not been challenged by those who have examined his time in office. However, Professor Harvie has expressed ambivalence regarding Johnston's centrist political approach and the 'cosy corporatism' it spawned;[37] and Professor

Smout has suggested that Johnston's administrative recourse to quangos and committees of experts has not yielded the kind of participatory democracy Scotland, in Smout's view, requires.[38]

Professor Harvie seems to regret Johnston's insistence that he was above party politics and that only a bi-partisan approach could bring results; he and many on the Scottish Left doubt whether Johnston was in any meaningful sense a socialist in his time as Secretary of State. Such a view is perhaps the product of an element of deceptiveness in Johnston throughout his career. For all the crusading journalism and his bouts of romanticism, Johnston was always a gradualist Socialist, happier travelling towards the objective of a socialist commonwealth than actually arriving at it. In his time at the Scottish Office it might be argued that this was still his basic philosophy: the way it was manifested in practice simply obscured its significance.

By repudiating party dogmas and political one-upmanship, it might be said that Johnston was not at the same time abandoning the essentially socialist objectives he had advanced throughout his career. For Johnston group exercises in co-operation and the pooling of ideas and resources were exercises which helped to bring a socialist society closer and to create a socialist political culture. They represented a 'common-sense' approach to the important questions of the day, and, in Johnston's lexicon, 'common-sense' and 'socialism' were synonymous. Johnston was indifferent to labels and definitional niceties. As Will Y. Darling wrote of him in his time at the Scottish Office: 'Gone, apparently, is the ardent propagandist of a political theory. He has no theories now – he asks if this is desirable, practical, worthwhile, and if so – on with it. Don't inquire – don't stop – don't write about it – don't harangue – don't ask if it is Christian or Marxian – on with it. This turbulent intensity commends itself to me.'[39] This was an apt summing-up not only of Johnston in the Scottish Office, but of Johnston the man and the practical Socialist. He had never in fact been a notable theorist, notwithstanding his voluminous writings on behalf of the Labour movement. He had always been basically guided by a strong pragmatism.

Johnston had long been an advocate of a socialism which grew from sensible administration and from co-operative experiments. The success of what he saw as democratic socialist policies in New Zealand and Sweden in the 1930s buoyed Johnston for similar developments in Britain. The main threat to such an outcome, in Johnston's estimation, were those on the Left who believed that things would have to get worse for the working class before a better socialist future could emerge. From John MacLean in 1910 to Stafford Cripps in the late 1930s Johnston rounded on those who advanced this 'theory of increasing misery'. His fundamental faith in progress never left him and it was his chief motivator in wartime.

Johnston had always been actuated by what he saw as the absurdities of capitalism; it did not make *sense*, in Johnston's view, to organise society along capitalist lines so that, for example food surpluses might be deliberately contrived only to be deliberately destroyed. If he was not, in wartime, bothered by definitions of socialism, Johnston certainly did not view welfareism, planning and public ownership as policies in the service of capitalism. He saw such policies simply as progress, progress to a more sensibly organised and run society, a poverty-less society, a society in which the energies and talents of the people would be released for the practical benefit of the community. These were precisely the objects he had always fought and campaigned for in the Labour movement and in his writings.

It can be said that Johnston desired a society and a political culture underpinned by values and assumptions of a collectivist, co-operative and practical socialist character. Group exercises of the sort he presided over in wartime were just the kind of tool to instil such values. There was no need, in Johnston's scheme of things, for class war, revolution, or the authoritarianism of Communism. If Conservatives went along with 'consensus' exercises then, in Johnston's outlook, perhaps this was only indicative of the extent to which society was moving in a sensible, and therefore socialist, direction. Johnston's enthusiasm for the teaching of citizenship in schools exemplifies his general outlook: a basic philosophy of caring for others and possessing a sense of duty to the community would ensure the betterment of all. While some would simply have labelled this 'humanitarian', it was the type of sentiment which had informed Johnston's socialism through the years. It would thus be perverse to disengage such views from a socialist ideal in respect of Johnston's wartime career, whatever the objections that might be raised about a flawed theoretical perspective invalidating claims to be Socialist. It mattered not that Johnston spurned party labels or declined to theorise; it was the consistency in outlook that was significant.

Johnston's priorities harmonised with the wartime atmosphere and with the major new political phenomenon of wartime Britain: Sir Richard Acland's Commonwealth. Like Acland, Johnston stressed notions of service to the community above all. The ideal of a socialist commonwealth was underpinned by that ethic of service he believed should be taught in schools and manifested in every walk of life. In Johnston's scheme of things everyone was a potential civil servant in the sense of fulfilling a duty to society. In her poem, 'The Cleansing of the Knife', Naomi Mitchison recollects Johnston's sentiments on a wartime visit to the fishing village of Carradale:

> We thirl ourselves to service
> From a free choice and wish.
> Tom Johnston said that day
> To the ring-net fishermen:
> 'Civil Servants catching fish'
> How many saw what lay

> Behind a phrase in a speech?
> Giving up old jealousies,
> Quarrels, suspicions, tricks,
> And the skippers' over-reach
> Of the share fishermen,
> For the different ethic of service.[40]

Professor Smout's observations on the alienation of the Scottish people from a quango-ridden administration after 1945 may be justified. It is less clear that the blame should be laid at Johnston's door. As Harvie has noted in connection with Smout's point, expertise did not necessarily imply elitism.[41] The last thing Johnston desired was government by an elite, or elites, and there was no sense in which his various councils and committees were infused with that spirit. Johnston was strongly in favour of local democratic decision-making as his defence of local government powers and his regional planning policies illustrate. He did not want to keep power at the centre, or in the hands of the few. Neither did he hold a concept of expertise which implied the participation of only a small number of people. Johnston believed that there were many kinds of expert, that all should be encouraged to get involved in decision-making, and that, crucially, the kind of experiments he introduced would have the effect of widening the range of expertise. His attempt to open up the education system to the scrutiny of a widely representative council was an example of his determination to foster cross-fertilisation and to open up Scottish society as much as was commensurate with its sound governance. Johnston's instincts remained democratic and, arguably, socialist in a way that the Labour Party's in Scotland in general did not.[42]

Above all Johnston's achievement was not doubted by the bulk of the Scottish people, and has not been since. 'Had Johnston', Professor Harvie has asked rhetorically, 'not simply restated the traditional dualism of post-union Scotland: the desire of its rulers to assimilate to the south, beneath a tartan smoke-screen?"[43] Did, then, Johnston desire this, did the Scottish people desire it also, or did the smokescreen, as suggested, deceive or console them?

The answer may be ambiguous but it may reflect yet more credit on Johnston's political instincts. For it is arguable that the Scots desired above all else that Scotland receive her fair share, be it of industrial production, planning powers, media coverage or anything else. While the majority of Scots had qualms about Home Rule and rejected separatism, they were adamant that they should not be cheated out of what was rightfully theirs within the framework of the UK. The Scots were more disposed in practice to the idea of reminding the English what Scotland was due as a partner, than to the idea of being independent. Johnston's successful efforts on Scotland's behalf thus aroused much admiration. Harvie has viewed some of Johnston's obsessions concerning apparently trivial matters as eccentric personal hobby horses.[44] However, chasing up such matters as Scottish banking uniforms being tailored, and Scottish telephone directories printed, in England, was exactly the kind of cause many Scots considered worthy and for which they would remember him. The idea of being assimilated to the south *was* objectionable to most Scots, but their nationalism in general extended only as far as applauding the apparent resistance to it that Johnston displayed. If this resistance was more apparent than real, and was understood as such by most Scots, then they were also prepared to be comforted by the 'tartan smokescreen' and its pride-salvaging properties.

Yet there was surely more than a smokescreen. Johnston achieved substantial gains for Scotland, and the Scottish people were suitably appreciative of the special treatment which he won for them in important areas such as planning, hydro-electricity and public health. Johnston gave many Scots a genuine sense of

Crucial Paradox.

pride in their country and the abilities of its people, and a greater awareness of its natural resources and products. The people believed Johnston when he told them that the Scottish voice was respected and listened to in London. Johnston had no Machiavellian intention or desire to blunt nationalist or Home Rule sentiment; on the contrary he believed, like he believed in gradual socialism, that Home Rule in greater measure would come all the sooner for the efficient working of the system as it stood. That the success of Johnston's schemes turned out to have the effect – after the war – of weakening the Home Rule cause,[45] was for reasons that had nothing to do with Johnston's own views and intentions. Johnston may have disliked the notion of a 'Sinn Fein' type separatism, but he always favoured Home Rule, and his Secretaryship of State was directed at achieving more of it and at creating the sound economic base he considered necessary for it.

Johnston preached self-help to his compatriots with unequivocal belief in their talents. Some, as Naomi Mitchison expresses it in verse, might have 'turned uneasily' before going 'back to sleep'. Others, like her, were inspired:

> And it seemed he might be the man
> Who could shake us surely awake and make us
> Lead ourselves, thirl ourselves to a service
> known and agreed
> And sing a new song.[46]

VI

Rumours abounded about Johnston's future after the end of the coalition Government. It was said that both Churchill and Attlee considered him a suitable choice for the post of viceroy of India. At such a momentous juncture in that country's history, it would have been the supreme challenge. Then there were whisperings about Johnston going to the House of Lords, rumours which persisted after he had formally turned down a peerage early in June 1945.

Such speculation was fuelled by the active role taken by Johnston in the election campaign. He was Labour's main spokesman in Scotland and was allocated one of the party's political broadcasts to argue the case for the maintenance of wartime economic controls. Although warmly praised by Churchill during the latter's Scotttish campaign stops, Johnston deplored in no uncertain terms Churchill's claim that the Labour Party would use 'Gestapo' tactics to enforce socialism. For Johnston, Churchill was bringing party fractiousness back into political life. It was this issue more than anything else which inspired him to campaign as strongly for Labour: he believed that they were the natural custodians of the new collectivist harmony which he and others had helped to construct during the war.

But Johnston himself was not entirely in harmony with the Labour Party. It was clear that the Party was firmly centralist in character and that Johnston would not be able, in the event of being Scottish Secretary in a Labour Government, to carry on schemes for separate Scottish development and reconstruction with the same degree of freedom of action and personal autonomy as he had enjoyed in the coalition. As Dr Paul Addison has pointed out, there was a contradiction between Labour's centralism and Johnston's appetite for separate Scottish agencies.[47]

In the event Labour won the election handsomely and Attlee presided over an administration bent on a centrally-planned future for a new egalitarian Britain. The power that mattered was the power of the State concentrated in London. It was not a context in which Johnston could have worked happily, however much he may have welcomed the historic Labour victory, the guarantee of the Welfare State, and other objectives for which he had long striven.

Johnston, then, probably viewed the prospect of continual

struggle on behalf of his Scottish plans as futile: far better to take an active part in consolidating and developing those agencies and institutions he had already brought into existence. He had not the remotest taste for further political scheming and plotting, whatever the probable rewards in terms of office and reputation. His concerns now were wholly focused on Scotland and on such areas of Scottish life as he, more than anyone, had influenced. This meant hydro-electricity and the development of the new North of Scotland Board; re-afforestation and the Scottish section of the Forestry Commission; and tourism and the new Scottish Tourist Board.

Johnston became chairman of the North of Scotland Hydro-Electric Board in April 1946 and continued in this capacity until 1959. In this time he used all his administrative, managerial, executive and public relations skills to establish hydro-electric schemes in many selected parts of the Highlands, including Loch Sloy, Loch Morar, and the Gairloch. He fought successfully to preserve the Board's independence when the electricity industry was nationalised by the Labour Government in 1947. The new schemes were a showcase for Scottish engineering, and they undoubtedly provided work and boosted the Highlands as an area of future industrial investment.

However, hydro-electricity could not of itself effect the repopulation of the Highlands which Johnston dreamed of – the reality was partial economic development, but little in the way of social and cultural 'recolonisation'.

Johnston also assumed the Chairmanship of the Scottish Committee of the Forestry Commission late in 1945. In this role he introduced a training scheme for those workers who came to forestry without rural experience, so that the industry would have wider appeal in respect of employment prospects. He presided over notable expansion; much privately-owned woodland was transferred to national forest service and more forestry-related commodities were home-grown rather than imported.

In his capacity of Chairman of the Scottish Tourist Board, a post he took up in December 1945, Johnston attempted to turn his advances in these former areas to the benefit of Scotland's overall appeal as an attractive country to visit, holiday in, and invest in. Johnston was just as exhaustive in his efforts to attract visitors to post-war Scotland as he was to attract war work in his time as Secretary of State. He launched vigorous publicity drives and paid particular attention to the task of improving accommodation for tourists: the new Highland amenities were stressed and forestry camps, among other things, were opened to visitors. This was Johnston in his element in this twilight chapter of his public life: getting down to the practicalities of advertising Scotland's attractions and attributes, from its angling facilities (which he himself continued to use) to its aura of historical romance.

His exclusive concern with Scottish issues led him to lose touch with British politics and the Labour Party. There is a suggestion, based on his support for John MacCormick's covenant movement for Scottish Home Rule in 1948 (which the Labour Party in Scotland steered clear of), that Johnston was more of a Scottish Nationalist than anything else after 1945. Certainly he continued to hold the view that Home Rule would assuredly come if Scotland proved itself able to make a success of its own economic life; and he remained convinced that Parliament would have to divest itself of some of its centralised functions. However, Johnston could not be said to have pressed for anything more than this type of piecemeal devolution, dispensed in stages by Westminster when it judged Scotland to be deserving of it. Nor was Johnston animated by any spirit of resentment or grievance against the British constitution and form of government, as he made clear at a speaking engagement in 1953: 'It may be that in Scotland the spirit of our people is outgrowing the forms of government which have hitherto been imposed upon us. Nevertheless, whatever the future may have in store, we in the twentieth century are proud that we are possessed of a Parliament in a democracy which is neither armed thuggery nor despotic decree.'[48]

In these later years of his life Johnston was fêted, by the normal standards of Scottish public acclaim, extravagantly. He was certainly not a prophet without honour in his own country. This reflected the very sincere appreciation of his compatriots for Johnston's decision to put Scotland before the personal rewards of politics. He was given the freedom of several towns and collected many academic and civic distinctions. In addition, he consented, in 1953, to accept the Companion of Honour at the request of Churchill.

Johnston was active in public life till the end of the 1950s. In retirement he suffered ill health and died at his home in Milngavie (close to Kirkintilloch) on 5 September 1965. He was eighty-three and left his wife and two daughters.

7 Conclusion

Johnston was the last outstanding Scottish Labour leader – Shinwell had lost touch with Scotland by 1945 and Maxton was in eclipse long before his death in 1946. Since 1945 the Labour movement in Scotland has struggled to give expression to that earlier radical spirit which blended potently the collectivist and the individualist strains so deeply embedded in Scottish life.[1] Hardie personified this spirit and Johnston was his worthiest successor. Both men were Socialists of a kind which was principled but not dogmatic, practical but not unromantic, far-seeing but not dreamlike, and flexible but not opportunist. Both men also were patriots, if not Nationalists.

This radical spirit was essentially a rural and small-town phenomenon. The 'egalitarian myth' carried more substance in such an environment than in the teeming cities where class divisions were far sharper.[2] This perhaps explains Johnston's 'phobia' about the city; his values, beliefs and hopes were less readily affirmed and nourished there. Perhaps too there was something of the despair of the middle-class reformer; municipal improvement was effected more easily where there were not masses of the destitute and the demoralised. But Johnston's vision for Scotland, for all its attractiveness, never entirely detached itself from a quasi-kailyard celebration of traditional Scottish virtues. Johnston never really addressed – indeed he may have been part of – Scotland's contradictions.

Johnston's instincts, at least from the 1920s, were towards political consensus and class harmony. He had put his pen at the service of raising the class-consciousness of the workers before and during the Great War, and class-conflict was not a concept he had shied from. However, the development of his thinking in the 1920s, especially in relation to the Empire, led him to identify socialist progress with consensual politics. In this he drew even closer to MacDonald, whose gradualist philosophy Johnston had always basically shared. There was more than a hint of irony in Johnston being associated with the 'honourable' wing of the Labour Cabinet in 1931, however sincere his stance over the cut in unemployment benefit. Johnston went on to operate the kind of consensual politics in the Second World War which MacDonald, rather naïvely, thought possible in 1931.

The 1930s was a period in which Johnston's outlook was less clear and some of his arguments less convincing than at any other point in his career. He was drawn in various directions on the subject of the economy, by turns emphasising export industries, domestic industries, public works, market surpluses at home and abroad, the machinations of high finance, and theories of a National Dividend. His interventions in these different areas were at times fruitful and always worthy of respect, and it would be unfair to condemn him for not fashioning a more coherent overall view; the economic complexities were formidable. However, a certain unsureness of touch perhaps lay behind his somewhat ambiguous behaviour in respect of Mosley's proposals and the economic policy of the Labour Government in 1930-31. Moreover, as the decade wore on his thinking on international issues was revealed as rather facile.

Johnston was in a good position in the Labour Party in the early 1930s, notwithstanding his electoral defeats in 1931 and 1932. It is an interesting, if hypothetical, question whether or not he might have become leader had he been in Parliament. His credentials were impeccable and his support in the Party strong. He had few, if any, enemies inside the Parliamentary Party. However, when he returned to Parliament late in 1935 the question simply did not arise. Johnston was still a major figure but he had not used the intervening years to further cultivate support, especially among the trade unions, or to take an active part in Labour Party affairs at national (British) level. Furthermore, he evidently did not possess the desire or the determination to become leader.

Johnston's achievements as Secretary of State for Scotland in wartime are, on the face of it, a reflection of the development of corporatism in government. Johnston's political outlook fitted very well into the corporatist model. Yet this tells only half the story. Johnston emphatically dissented from the deification of centralisation as the natural accompaniment to the new collectivist approach. Arguably his brand of socialism was responsible for this: it was commonsensical and piecemeal, but it was also locally-based and infused with the spirit of self-help. Johnston may have also recognised that the socialist impulse was liable to be blunted in a corporatist context in which capital spoke loudest and spoke, increasingly, in favour of monopolies. Johnston's position in the planning mainstream from the early 1930s had never been a centralist one. He had always wanted to apply planning principles and concepts locally and to wed them to notions of participatory democracy. His outlook always owed much to the vision of Scotland he had cherished since his earliest years in politics: a vibrant, small nation full of self-supporting small communities.

Johnston's political exit in 1945 was at once fitting and tantalising. He bowed out with an illustrious record as a politician and a journalist behind him. Yet he also left unresolved some important issues of political principle. He did not, for example, develop a critique of centralisation in relation to Scotland, or provide a defence of his decentralist approach in relation to the fashionable socialist wisdom of the day. He detested unwieldy bureaucratic structures yet made no public protest at the Labour Party's apparent tendency towards them. It may have benefited the Labour Party in Scotland and the people of Scotland if he had made clear where he stood on such issues before he left the political stage.

Johnston also declined to relate his ideas about Scotland's future to the awkward reality of the country's divisions. Both in wartime and afterwards Johnston, more than anyone, had the respect and admiration of the Scottish people and could have used it to set the agenda for debate and self-examination. He might have tried to encourage Scots to confront and to work out the cultural and social tensions which were – and are – so notable. These would have entailed the social tensions between Protestants and Catholics; the cultural gulf between the High-lands and Lowlands; and the division between urban and rural Scotland and their conflicting economic interests and needs. Johnston certainly did not waste his later years, and, indeed, he continued to do much practical good for Scotland. However, given that his mind was still working powerfully, this might have been an opportunity to help Scotland which he did not take.

In the final reckoning such criticism seems almost churlish. Johnston was, without equivocation, an admirable man. He was selfless and magnanimous and, although reserved, humorous and warm. He was never a natural politician, although his achieve-ments in that capacity were considerable. He was, more naturally, a propagandist and an administrator, and his talents in both areas were brought together in his practical socialism. He was a 'doer' rather than a theorist, but also a man of ideas who played an important role in the Labour movement in Britain as a whole in refining, clarifying and presenting cogently much of the thinking of his times. He was a catalyst figure whose presence rubbed off productively on those around him. And he was a man of genuine vision, inspired by a healthy and dignified patriotism.

Notes

Chapter 1

1 C. Harvie, *No Gods and Precious Few Heroes* (London, 1981).

2 T. Johnston, *Memories* (London, 1952), p. 31.

3 *Forward*, 4 January 1913.

4 See F. Reid, 'Keir Hardie and *Labour Leader*', in J. M. Winter, *The Working Class in Modern British History* (Cambridge, 1983).

5 Prospectus in Emrys Hughes papers, NLS Dep. 176 Box 26.

6 E. Hughes, 'Left over the border', *The Guardian* 1 April 1960.

7 *Forward*, 27 October 1906.

8 *Ibid.*, 30 April 1910.

9 See P. Clarke, 'The social democratic theory of the class struggle', in Winter, *op. cit.*

10 *Forward*, 4 June 1910.

11 T. Johnston, *The Case for Women's Suffrage and Objections Answered* (Glasgow, 1908).

12 T. Johnston and H. Adams, *The Railway Difficulty and How to Solve It* (Glasgow, 1908).

13 *Forward*, 27 June 1908.

14 *Ibid.*, 25 September 1909.

15 *Ibid.*, 9 October 1909.

16 *Ibid.*, 23 February 1907.

17 *Ibid.*, 25 June 1910.

18 J. Smith, 'Labour tradition in Glasgow and Liverpool', *History Workshop*, 17 (Spring 1984) pp. 32-56.

19 D. Howell, *British Workers and the Independent Labour Party* (Manchester, 1983) p. 140.

20 *Forward*, 9 September 1909.

21 *Ibid.*, 21 December 1912.

22 *Ibid.*, 9 July to 24 September 1910.

23 See K. O. Morgan, *Keir Hardie, Radical and Socialist* (London, 1975), pp. 288-9.

24 See J. R. MacDonald, *Socialism and Government* (London, 1909).

25 *Forward*, 6 April 1912.
26 *Ibid.,* 3 February 1912.

Chapter 2

1 *Forward*, 8 August 1914.
2 *Ibid.*, 22 August 1914.
3 *Secret Diplomacy, Capitalism and War* (Glasgow, 1914).
4 *Forward*, 26 September 1914.
5 *Ibid.*, 23 January 1915.
6 See the entry on Johnston in W. Knox (ed.) *Scottish Labour Leaders 1918-39* (Edinburgh, 1984).
7 *Forward*, 19 September 1914.
8 *Ibid.*, 12 December 1914.
9 *Loc. cit.*
10 Johnston, in a later defence of MacDonald, said that the end he had in mind was not that of the militarists. *Forward*, 10 April 1915.
11 *Forward*, 2 January 1915. Hardie, however, also made 'see it through' utterances. See K. O. Morgan, *Keir Hardie* (London, 1975) p. 266.
12 *Forward*, 28 August 1915.
13 *Ibid.*, 2 October 1915.
14 W. Gallacher, *Revolt on the Clyde* (London, 1936), p. 99.
15 *Forward*, 11 December 1915.
16 T. Johnston, *Memories* (London, 1952) p. 38.
17 *Forward*, 1 January 1916.
18 *Loc. cit.*
19 *Forward*, 5 February 1916.
20 See T. Brotherstone, 'The suppression of the *Forward*', *Scottish Labour History Society Journal* 1 (1969) pp. 5-23; and J. Hinton, 'The suppression of the *Forward* – a note', *Scottish Labour History Society Journal*, 7 (1973) pp. 4-9.
21 Brotherstone, *op. cit.*
22 Iain McLean, *The Legend of Red Clydeside* (Edinburgh, 1983), pp. 61-2.
23 *Forward*, 17 June 1916.
24 *Ibid.*, 10 March 1917.
25 *Ibid.*, 17 March 1917.
26 *Loc. cit.*
27 *Forward*, 3 November 1917.
28 *Ibid.*, 8 September 1917.
29 *Ibid.*, 2 November 1918.

30 *Ibid.*, 22 September 1917.

31 *Ibid.*, 1 June 1918.

32 *Ibid.*, 4 January 1919.

33 *Ibid.*, 15 February 1919.

34 *Ibid.*, 20 September 1919.

35 Not, however, John MacLean, who turned his sights on a 'Scottish Workers' Republic'.

36 *Forward*, 14 August 1920.

37 *Ibid.*, 31 July 1920.

38 I. C. G. Hutchinson, *A Political History of Scotland 1832-1924* (Edinburgh, 1986), p. 278.

39 *Forward*, 13 November 1920.

40 See *ibid.*, 9 July 1921.

41 *Ibid.*, 20 August 1921.

42 See A. Reid, 'Glasgow socialism', *Social History*, II 1 (January 1986), pp. 89-97.

43 See J. Melling, *Rent Strikes* (Edinburgh, 1983), pp. 23, 33.

44 See McLean, *op. cit., passim.*

45 See R. J. Morris, 'Skilled workers and the politics of the "Red" Clyde: a discussion paper', *Scottish Labour History Society Journal*, 18 (1983).

46 Muirhead papers, Acc. 3721 Box 149(4). This is the source for the information on *Forward* which follows.

47 See E. Hughes, 'Left over the border', *The Guardian*, 1 April 1960.

48 Quoted in *Forward*, 24 April 1920.

49 See T. C. Smout, *A Century of the Scottish People* (London, 1986). p. 267.

50 *Forward*, 18 May 1918.

Chapter 3

1 159 H.C. Deb., C. 141-4 (23 November 1922).

2 *Forward*, 7 July 1923.

3 T. Henderson, The *Scottish Socialists* (London, 1931) p. 129.

4 *Forward* 17 November 1923.

5 Emrys Hughes Papers, NLS Dep. 176 Box 10(1).

6 *Forward*, 31 May 1924.

7 *Ibid.*, 26 July 1924.

8 174 H.C. Deb., C. 2040-43 (17 June 1924).

9 T. Johnston, *Memories* (London, 1952) p. 54.

10 *New Leader*, 26 June 1925.

11 *Forward*, 17 May 1924.
12 *Ibid.*, 1 September 1923.
13 *Ibid.*, 17 May 1924.
14 *Ibid.*, 1 November 1924.
15 *Ibid.*, 17 October 1925.
16 For a critical appraisal of this visit see G. Douds, 'Tom Johnston in India', *Journal of the Scottish Labour History Society*, 19 (1984), pp. 6-21.
17 *Forward*, 2 January 1926.
18 Johnston, *op. cit.*, p. 71.
19 *Forward*, 2 January 1926.
20 H.C. Deb., c. 1515 (25 March 1926).
21 *Forward*, 14 August 1926.
22 198 H.C. Deb., C. 2425 (29 July 1926).
23 British Commonwealth Labour Conference Report 1928, Labour Party Archives.
24 J. Adam Smith, *John Buchan* (Oxford, 1985) p. 318.
25 *Forward*, 23 August 1924.
26 *Ibid.*, 22 August 1925.
27 MacDonald to Johnston 22 January 1927, MacDonald papers, PRO 30/69 (1172).
28 *Forward*, 8 October 1927.
29 *Ibid.*, 7 January 1928.
30 *Ibid.*, 11 August 1928.
31 See H. Dalton, *Call Back Yesterday* (London, 1953), pp. 213-14, and Johnston, *op. cit.*, pp. 100-1.

Chapter 4

1 *Forward*, 15 June 1929.
2 *Ibid.*, 18 January 1930.
3 *Ibid.*, 15 November 1930.
4 See T. Johnston, *Memories* (London, 1952), pp. 100-1, and G. Pottinger, *The Secretaries of State for Scotland* (Edinburgh, 1979) pp. 43-5.
5 See R. Skidelsky, *Politicians and the Slump* (London, 1967), pp. 402-3.
6 *Ibid.*, p. 91.
7 Johnston, *op. cit.*, p. 106. See also Johnston's letter to MacDonald, 24 January 1930, CAB 24/209 C.P. 33(30).
8 CAB 27/389, D.U. (29), 6th conclusions, 8 October 1929.
9 See CAB 27/391.

10 B. Pimlott (ed.), *The Political Diaries of Hugh Dalton* (London, 1986), p. 111.

11 Thomas Jones, *Whitehall Diary*, Vol. II (London, 1969), pp. 259-60.

12 CAB 24/209, C.P. 33(30).

13 239 H.C. Deb., C. 1387-94.

14 Jones, *op. cit.*, p. 260.

15 A. Booth and M. Pack, *Employment, capital and economic policy* (Oxford, 1985), p. 4.

16 MacDonald Papers, PRO 30/69 (1176).

17 See for example, H. Dalton, *Call Back Yesterday* (London, 1953), p. 235.

18 251 H.C. Deb., C. 375-88.

19 CAB 23/67, 17 June 1931.

20 CAB 23/67, 19 August 1931.

21 See P. Williamson, 'A bankers' ramp? Financiers and the British political crisis of August 1931', *English Historical Review*, 99 (1984), pp. 770-806.

22 See Williamson, *op. cit.*, 803. Johnston knew that MacDonald did not require to be dictated to on the question of unemployment benefit cuts. In his memoirs (p. 108) Johnston admits that there was no bankers' plot.

23 *Forward*, 5 September 1931.

24 256 H.C. Deb., C. 478.

25 Goronwy Rees, in his *Great Slump* (London, 1970, pp. 189-90), attributes to Johnston the often-quoted response, 'they never told us we could do that'. There is no certain evidence that Johnston or any other ex-minister actually did say this, but it is indicative of the Labour Cabinet's acceptance of the view that it could not tamper with the gold standard.

26 *Forward*, 9 January 1932.

27 *Ibid.*, 30 January 1932.

28 See all issues of *Forward* during July 1932.

29 *Forward*, 7 January 1933.

30 T. Johnston, *Financiers and the Nation* (London, 1934), p. 125.

31 *Ibid.*, p. 200.

32 See, for example, *Forward*, 20 April 1935.

33 *Ibid.*, 30 March 1935.

34 H. Dalton, *The Fateful Years* (London, 1957), p. 25.

35 B. Pimlott, *op. cit.*, pp. 74-5, 98.

Chapter 5

1 For the Ponsonby–Johnston debate see *Forward*, 25 January 1936.

2 *Forward*, 4 January 1936.

3 *Ibid.*, 3 October 1936. Rangers won the match 2-1.

4 *Glasgow Herald*, 29 September 1936.

5 *Ibid.*, 19 October 1936.

6 Hughes Papers, NLS Dep. 176 Box 26(2).

7 *Glasgow Herald*, 16 December 1936.

8 *Forward*, 4 June 1938.

9 M. Keating and D. Bleiman, *Labour and Scottish Nationalism* (London, 1979), pp. 126-7.

10 *Forward*, 4 June 1938.

11 Johnston, like the majority in the Labour Party, held aloof from them.

12 *Forward*, 24 September 1938.

13 344 H.C. Deb., C. 1602-3.

14 See *Forward*, 25 March 1939, and *Fortnightly*, May 1939.

15 T. Johnston, *Memories*, pp. 134-5.

16 PRO, HO 186/79.

17 See *Forward*, 8 July 1939.

18 PRO, HO 186/1462.

19 *Glasgow Herald*, 2 December 1939.

20 B. Pimlott (ed.), *The Political Diaries of Hugh Dalton*, p. 316.

21 *Glasgow Herald*, 13 January 1941.

22 *Loc. cit.*

23 *Glasgow Herald*, 30 January 1941.

24 Johnston, *op. cit.*, pp. 147-8.

Chapter 6

1 H. J. Hanham, 'The development of the Scottish Office', in J. J. Wolfe (ed.), *Government and Nationalism in Scotland* (Edinburgh, 1969), pp. 67-8. pp. 67-8.

2 C. Harvie, 'Labour and Scottish government: the age of Tom Johnston', *The Bulletin of Scottish Politics*, 2 (Spring 1981), pp. 1-20.

3 Will Y. Darling, *King's Cross to Waverley* (London, 1942), p. 42.

4 Muirhead papers, NLS Acc. 3721 Box 3 (59).

5 *Glasgow Herald*, 17 February 1942.

6 SRO HH50/166,

7 J. C. W. Reith, *Into the Wind* (London, 1949), pp. 431-3, and *Glasgow Herald*, 7 March 1942.

8 SRO HH50/166.

9 SRO HH50/168.

10 SRO HH50/169.

11 SRO HH50/170.

12 *Glasgow Herald*, 13 and 16 May 1942.

13 *Ibid.*, 1 December 1942.

14 See cabinet memorandum, 23 February 1944, CAB 87/7, R(44), 32.

15 See J. Lloyd, 'Tom Johnston's parliament on education: the birth of the sixth Advisory Council on Education in Scotland 1942-3', *Scottish Educational Review*, 16 (2) 1984, pp. 104-15.

16 410 H.C. Deb., C. 1267 (1 May 1945).

17 See Lloyd, *op. cit.*.

18 T. Johnston, *Memories*, pp. 153-4.

19 391 H.C. Deb., C. 937 (21 July 1943).

20 CAB 65/36 (1 December 1943).

21 408 H.C. Deb., C. 259 (14 February 1945).

22 H.Morrison, *Autobiography* (London, 1960), p. 199.

23 See Harvie, *op. cit.*, n. 41.

24 CAB 65/41 (15 February 1944).

25 CAB 87/7, R(44)2.

26 CAB 87/5, R(44), 10 January 1944.

27 Cmd. 6502. See J. E. Pater, *The Making of the National Health Service* (London, 1981), pp. 70-2.

28 CAB 87/5, R(44), 11 January 1944.

29 SRO, HH50/181.

30 Pater, *op. cit.*, pp. 70-2.

31 CAB 87/8, R(44) 122.

32 *Ibid.*, R(44) 125.

33 C. Barnett, *The Audit of War* (London, 1986), *passim*.

34 *Glasgow Herald*, 6 January 1945.

35 *Ibid.* 24 May 1945.

36 SRO HH50/177. See also C. Harvie, 'Labour in Scotland in the Second World War', *Historical Journal*, 26, 4 (1983), pp. 921-44.

37 Harvie, 'Labour and Scottish government'.

38 T. C. Smout, *A Century of the Scottish People*, pp. 272-3.

39 Darling, *op. cit.*, p. 42.

40 N. Mitchison, *The Cleansing of the Knife* (Edinburgh, 1978), p. 70.

41 *The Scotsman*, 31 May 1986.

42 Smout, *op. cit.* pp. 274-5.

43 Harvie, 'Labour and Scottish government'.

44 *Loc. cit.*
45 M. Keating and D. Bleiman, *Labur and Scottish Nationalism*, pp. 129-30.
46 Mitchison, *op. cit.*, p. 71.
47 This point was made in a BBC Scotland Radio programme on Tom Johnston written and presented by Christopher Harvie in 1981.
48 *Glasgow Herald*, 15 October 1953.

Chapter 7

1 See article by Jimmy Reid, *New Statesman*, 19 June 1987.
2 See A. McPherson, 'An angle on the geist: persistance and change in the Scottish educational tradition', in W. M. Humes and H. M. Paterson (eds.), *Scottish Culture and Scottish Education* (Edinburgh, 1983).

A note on further reading

Primary sources

There are two collections of Johnston's private papers, one in the National Library of Scotland (NLS, Acc.5862) in Edinburgh, and one in the Mitchell Library, Glasgow (G.880261). Both are rather disappointing.

Johnston's publicatons – books and pamphlets – are held by the Mitchell Library and the NLS, and *A History of the Working Classes in Scotland* is widely available in public and college libraries. The *Forward* can be consulted at the Mitchell, the NLS and the British Newspaper Library at Colindale in London.

The Government and Cabinet papers used here, as well as the Ramsay MacDonald Papers, are to be found in the Public Record Office (PRO) in Kew, London. Scottish Office papers, including the minutes of the Council of State 1942-45 (filed under the Home and Health Department) are in the Scottish Record Office (SRO) in Edinburgh. Relevant Labour Party material cited in the footnotes is held in the Party archives in Walworth Road, London. Three especially useful collections of private papers, those of Emrys Hughes, Arthur Woodburn and Roland Muirhead, are in the NLS.

Secondary sources

Of the scholarly works cited in the footnotes, those by Harvie, Smout and MacLean are particularly recommended. Michael Fry's *Patronage and Principle: A Political History of Modern Scotland* (1987) appeared too late for consideration; it presents a different view of Johnston's Secretaryship from 1941-45 than the one offered here, and is generally a rewarding read. Memoirs such as Fenner Brockway's *Inside the Left* (1942), David Kirkwood's *My Life of Revolt* (1935), Harry McShane's *No Mean Fighter* (1978), and W. M. Haddow's *My Seventy Years* (1943) convey a flavour of the world Johnston moved in. T. J. Honeyman's *Art and Audacity* (1971) makes some pertinent points about Johnston in relation to the Scottish tourist industry.

Index

Index

Index